ANANDA COURSE IN SELF-REALIZATION

Lessons in Meditation

ANANDA COURSE IN SELF-REALIZATION

Lessons in Meditation

*Based on the Teachings of Paramhansa Yogananda
And His Direct Disciple, Swami Kriyananda*

Jyotish Novak

Crystal Clarity Publishers
Nevada City, California

Crystal Clarity Publishers, Nevada City, CA 95959
Copyright © 2009, 2006, 1997 by Hansa Trust
First edition 1997. Second edition 2006. Third edition 2009
All rights reserved. Published 2009
Printed in the USA
ISBN: 978-1-56589-177-7

*Cover photograph and design by Barbara Bingham, produced by Crystal
Clarity Publishers. Interior layout and design by Crystal Clarity Publishers.*

*Ananda Church of Self-Realization was founded in 1968 by
Swami Kriyananda, a direct disciple of Paramhansa Yogananda.
We are not affiliated with Self-Realization Fellowship.*

Library of Congress Cataloging-in-Publication Data

Novak, John (John Jyotish)
   Lessons in Meditation : Based on the Teachings of Paramhansa Yogananda and His
Direct Disciple Swami Kriyananda / by Jyotish Novak ; Ananda Course in Self-
Realization presented by Ananda Sangha Worldwide. — 3rd ed.
      p. cm.
   ISBN 978-1-56589-177-7 (tradepaper)
   1. Meditation. 2. Self-realization. 3. Yogananda, Paramhansa, 1893-1952. 4. Kri-
yananda, Swami. I. Ananda Sangha (Organization) II. Title.
   BL627.N68 2009
   294.5'435—dc22   2009028989

www.crystalclarity.com
800.424.1055
clarity@crystalclarity.com

Contents

Introduction

A Course in Yoga

You are about to embark on a marvelous journey, a journey to the unexplored center of your own self. Along the way you will discover you have strengths and potentials you only dimly suspected.

Yoga is an ancient science; so ancient, in fact, that its roots are lost in the dim reaches of time. We know that it goes back at least seven thousand years because of prehistoric stone tablets found at Mohenjo Daro in India depicting people in yoga postures. There is a continuous tradition several thousand years old of scriptural writings on yoga. And yet it is not merely some hoary philosophy left dusty and tattered by the passage of time. It is a living tradition! It has been practiced continuously and refined over centuries. In India every generation has had its saints and sages. In the twentieth century there have been several great yogis who have reached the highest possible state of awareness: Self-realization.

The Sanskrit word *yoga* means union. In one sense this union implies a complete integration of our own self, a total clarity of consciousness. In more expanded states, the yogi experiences a state of union with every atom of creation. In a spiritual sense, the yogi achieves a state of union in which the individual soul merges into God.

But long before you experience these profound states you will find extraordinary benefits from practicing the lessons in this course. Physically, you will experience increasing vitality, flexibility, and strength. Mentally you will be able to work with more clarity and concentration. Your emotions also will benefit—you'll become more even-minded, learn to overcome negative moods, and develop attitudes which bring true happiness and well-being. You will rediscover a sense of peace and harmony with the world around you, and your capacity to give and receive love will expand until it embraces all places and every living thing. Finally, you will find a joy so profound that it will seem to form the very fabric of creation itself. Great truths lie within you at this very moment. You have only to still your restless thoughts to find all this and more.

Paramhansa Yogananda
and the Ananda Tradition

The material in this course is based on the teachings of
Paramhansa Yogananda. He was one of the first yogis, and
perhaps the greatest, ever to live and teach in the United
States. Yogananda came to America in 1920 in order to address
the Council of Religious Liberals in Boston. He stayed on to
write, lecture, and give classes in yoga. Within a few years
he became an enormously popular figure. His classes were
so well received that crowds had to be turned away even at
America's largest auditoriums, such as Carnegie Hall in New
York. But Yogananda was far beyond being enamored of
popularity. He came to this country not for fame but simply
to offer the soul-liberating teachings of yoga. In the mid-
1930s he moved to Los Angeles and established a center to
spread these teachings. It was here that he wrote his classic
book *Autobiography of a Yogi*, which has introduced millions to the wonders of yoga.

Ananda was started by Swami Kriyananda, a direct
disciple of Yogananda. Kriyananda lived with Yogananda
from 1948 until the great master's passing in 1952. Charged
by Yogananda to do his utmost to make these teachings
available, Kriyananda has spent his life teaching, writing,
and working in countless ways to serve his guru. He has
written over one hundred books and more than four
hundred pieces of music, but perhaps his greatest work
was the founding of Ananda World Brotherhood Village.
Ananda is widely considered to be one the most successful
spiritual communities in the world. It has grown to include

one hundred meditation groups around the world, as well as seven branch communities. More than one thousand resident members live a life based on yogic principles. Ananda has become a living laboratory to test the effectiveness of the teachings presented in these lessons.

How These Courses Are Organized

The *Ananda Course in Self-Realization* is designed to give you complete instruction and a groundwork for the practice of meditation, yoga postures, and the yogic path.

The Four Stages

There are four stages to the *Ananda Course in Self-Realization*. First come seven lessons entitled *Lessons in Meditation*. In this first stage you will learn the basic techniques of meditation as taught by Paramhansa Yogananda. You will also learn the *Energization Exercises*, his unique contribution to the science of yoga. Each lesson contains the following sections: Principles, Techniques, Routine, and Do This Now, which is a homework assignment. A typical student takes a week or two to complete each lesson.

Stage two of the course is *The Art and Science of Yoga: 14 Steps to Higher Awareness*. Here the emphasis shifts to a much deeper understanding of the philosophy of yoga and a thorough presentation of *hatha yoga*, the yoga postures. Each of the lessons contains seven elements: Philosophy of Yoga, Yoga Postures, Breathing, Routine, Healing Principles and Techniques, Diet, and Meditation, where some of the techniques learned in stage one are reviewed and placed in their broader context. By the end of this stage you will not only have a complete background in the science and art of yoga, but you will understand how it can be applied to all aspects of your life.

Stage three, *Discipleship*, gives you the opportunity to learn about the guru-disciple relationship and, should you choose, to become a disciple of Paramhansa Yogananda. You are then eligible to learn his advanced technique of AUM meditation.

Finally, stage four, *Kriya Preparation*, prepares you for initiation into Paramhansa Yogananda's most advanced technique, Kriya Yoga. Paramhansa Yogananda described Kriya Yoga as the "jet airplane" path to God.

Self-Effort

This course is designed to let you proceed at a pace that feels natural and comfortable. But it will require effort on your part. Meditation and deeper spiritual states must be experienced, not merely read about. They can't be appreciated by mere reading any more than an orange can be tasted by only *studying* its qualities. How much effort is involved? This you must decide for yourself. But any effort you make will pay dividends very quickly. From the very start you will feel more relaxed, more cheerful, and more at peace with yourself. All areas of your life can improve with a surprisingly small amount of effort—less than half an hour per day to start with.

May these lessons bring you great joy!

Ananda Sangha Worldwide is a dynamic organization with many teachers who have lived and taught these practices for 40 years or more. If you have any questions about the course material, or simply want to talk to someone, we are here to help you.

Ananda Course Support

course@ananda.org
530.470.2340
www.ananda.org/meditation/course

14618 Tyler Foote Road, #145
Nevada City, CA 95959

Ananda Sangha Worldwide

www.ananda.org
sanghainfo@ananda.org

GETTING STARTED

Lesson 1

Principles

What Is Meditation?

Meditation is a state of intense awareness achieved by stilling and concentrating the thoughts. It is a journey to the center of our own being, a process so perfectly natural that we don't have to learn how to meditate. Rather, we have to unlearn those habits and attitudes that keep us from experiencing our natural state of expanded awareness. We simply need to still the mental restlessness which, like static on a radio, prevents us from hearing clearly our own natural "program." Deeper states of meditation come automatically as we peel away the layers of tension and attachments that prevent us from being more aware.

Meditation, like science, is based upon experimentation. Rather than indoctrinating us with a rigid dogma, it says, "Try this and see what the results are." Science discovers truths about nature, while meditation allows us to learn truths about our own nature. Since consciousness cannot be accurately observed from outside itself, we must find a way for consciousness to observe itself. In fact, self-observation is a good definition of meditation. When you meditate, adopt the methods of a scientist. Your tools, rather than microscopes and oscilloscopes, are concentration and intuition.

Meditation is not "thinking deep thoughts." In fact, true meditation begins only when thinking ends. To progress in meditation we must put aside the mental tendency to constantly seek out and solve problems, to worry and plan, to react and judge. While we are meditating we need to let go of the past and future.

Meditation is not passive, it requires energy and commitment! But it is not physical work either. In meditation, effort must be applied in a direction opposite to what we are used to. Our "effort" must be to relax ever more deeply. We must ultimately release the tension from both our muscles and our thoughts. Meditation requires, above all, complete attention.

Meditation is not letting the mind drift in a subconscious state or float in pleasant daydreams. It is a state of high energy, of intense awareness. If, at the end of a meditation, you don't know what happened, then you weren't really meditating. Meditation raises us above both the dreamy subconsciousness and the restless conscious mind. It brings us in touch with the superconscious state—acutely aware, intuitively certain. Profound perceptions come from the superconscious rather than the conscious mind. When we relax so deeply that we are able to internalize the energy of the senses, the mind becomes focused and a tremendous flow of energy is awakened. That intense energy lifts us into superconsciousness, where our powers of intuition are fully awake. In superconsciousness we become aware of realities barely dreamed of before.

While meditation is a continuous process, it can be said to have three stages: relaxation, interiorization, and expansion. Put very simply, the process of meditation could be described as:

a) relaxing the body and the mind,

b) concentrating single-pointedly on the object of your meditation, and

c) expanding your sense of identity until you realize your unity with all creation.

Paramhansa Yogananda defined meditation as "deep concentration on God or one of His aspects." As you concentrate on God you begin to realize, as all Scriptures teach, that you are made in His image. You are a child of God and His kingdom lies within. His qualities are your qualities. His peace is your peace. His universal love is yours to taste and to offer to all the world. His joy can make life a priceless gift. Deeper states such as these do not come easily, however. They require dedication and discipline. And yet, even a little meditation has profound rewards. India's great Scripture, the *Bhagavad Gita*, says, "Even a little practice of this inward religion will save one from dire fears and colossal suffering."

Meditation and Health

Meditation has great health benefits. It is one of the best possible antidotes to the excessive stress of modern life. Stress pushes the body into a "fight or flight" response. This can be valuable for short-term survival, but over the long run, the resulting hormonal response can cause serious health problems. Meditation gives us a respite from pressure. As we relax, the heart beats more slowly and the blood pressure lowers. Meditation helps retrain response mechanisms so we don't react as strongly or as negatively to adverse situations. It gives us the ability to be more centered, to be more in control of ourselves.

Meditation has been found to strengthen the immune system, which helps ward off diseases before they affect us and lets us recover more quickly when we do become ill. Much has been written recently about the mind-body connection. Meditation helps create a healthy mind, one that is alert, positive, and calm. This, in turn, produces a body filled with vitality and health. A master of yoga can control even autonomic processes such as heart rate, pulse, and brain waves.

A meditative life helps foster other aspects of a healthy life style. The medical establishment has finally recognized that general health can be greatly improved by a combination of meditation, proper diet, and yoga postures. Dr. Dean Ornish has shown that even serious heart and circulatory problems can be reversed through a careful regime of diet, meditation, and exercise. Perhaps the ultimate sign of mainstream acceptance is that some insurance companies are now paying for patients to learn how to meditate.

Meditation also helps foster a healthy mind. It allows us to release negative mental states such as fear, worry, and anger and replace them with positive attitudes. The daily practice of focusing within gradually gives us control over the flow of life-force, letting us turn it inward. As a result, we feel more fulfilled and lose the addiction to constantly seeking satisfaction from things outside ourselves: from possessions, or endless entertainment, or drugs and alcohol. The simple reversal of the direction of life-force has dramatic results. Far from becoming bored or life-negating, we regain our ability to find enjoyment in simple pleasures.

During this home-study course you will learn techniques to consciously control the flow of energy (life-force). This can be used as a powerful healing tool. A member of the Ananda community had a remarkable experience in this regard. He was hiking alone on a glacier in Canada. During the morning he had gone out several miles, intending to reverse directions after lunch and arrive home safely before sunset. But, just as he started his return trip, he slipped and badly sprained his ankle. Unable to walk, or even to stand, he knew the situation was serious, unprepared as he was to spend a night out on the ice. Knowing the yogic technique of energization (which you will learn in Lesson Six) he sent life-force to his swollen ankle. After a few minutes the pain began to subside and after a half-hour he was able to resume walking. He has always felt that he owes his life to the healing principles of energy control.

Techniques

When to Meditate

For the vast majority of people the best times to meditate are in the morning just after waking and in the evening before going to bed. But meditation can be done any time and anywhere you can be quiet and inward.

Plan to meditate every day. Try meditating fifteen to twenty minutes twice a day in the beginning. You can gradually increase the time, but don't go beyond your capacity to enjoy each meditation. Depth of focus is much more important than merely increasing the amount of time. As you progress it is natural to want to meditate longer, and the more you meditate, the more you will want to meditate!

Choose a convenient time for your meditations. Regularity is the most important factor, so find a time when you can be consistent. Creating a *habit* of meditation is far and away the most important goal in the beginning. Most people find that early morning and late evening are the times most under their control and the least likely to have other demands. These times are important for other reasons also. In the morning the mind is quieter, not yet engaged in the busyness of the day. It is easiest to reprogram the subconscious mind, where habits are rooted, just after or just before sleep. Also, at these times the thoughts of people around us are calmer and less disturbed. It is best to wait at least a half hour after eating—up to three hours after a heavy meal—so there will not be competition for energy between digestion and meditation.

Many people also like to meditate before lunch or right after work. Meditating at these times breaks the cycle of endless activity and gets you centered again. A friend who worked as a nurse in an emergency ward was a near legend among her coworkers for her ability to stay centered in every situation. She credited her calmness to her habit of meditating at lunch and briefly during her breaks.

Where to Meditate

If possible, set aside an area that is used only for meditation. This will help create a meditative mood and, over time, your special place will become filled with meditation "vibrations." A small room or closet is ideal as long as it can be well ventilated. If you don't have enough space for a whole room, then set aside a small area in your bedroom or some other room that can be reserved for meditation. If you can, face east as you meditate. This helps to align the magnetism of your body with that of the earth.

Your meditation area can be kept very simple—all you really need is a chair or small cushion to sit on. You can enhance the mood by creating a small altar with pictures of those holy ones who inspire you. Many people also like to have a small candle and an incense burner. Your altar can be as simple or elaborate as you like. In any case, your real altar is your heart.

It is good, occasionally, to meditate outside in nature, but this should be the exception rather than the rule. Deep meditation demands complete interiorization. There is, in fact, a stage in meditation called *pratyahara,* which means to interiorize even the senses. Yogananda referred to this as "shutting off the sense telephones." So choose a quiet place for your meditation area, a place where you can concentrate without distractions.

Being able to shut out sounds will help your meditations. You can purchase inexpensive earplugs at any pharmacy or sporting goods store. Simple rubber earplugs can be very effective, but some people find them uncomfortable for longer meditations. If this is true for you, try foam earplugs. They don't block sounds quite as well, but they are very comfortable. You can also use earphones made to reduce industrial noise. These are very effective and often the choice of long-time meditators. If you have difficulty finding any of these products, write or call us at the number given at the start of this course, and we can help you.

Posture

There are many ways of sitting for meditation that are equally good. You can sit either in a straight-backed chair or on the floor in any of several poses. Two things, however, are essential: Your spine must be straight, and you must be able to relax completely.

Proper Posture for Sitting in a Chair

Choose a chair with a straight back and a padded seat. Sit away from the back of the chair, so there is no pressure on your spine, and place your hands palms upright at the junction of the thighs and the abdomen. Bring your shoulders back a little in order to keep from slumping. Some people find this a little awkward at first, but they soon get used to it. A straight spine is important for complete relaxation. If you slump, skeletal muscles must tense to help support your weight, and a bent spine inhibits the flow of the subtle energies necessary for deeper states. Keep the chest up—you might try feeling that there is a line attached to the chest pulling it upward and forward at a 45 degree angle. The chin should be kept level with the floor.

You may find it helpful to place a woolen blanket or silk cloth or both over your chair. Yogis recommend this to block certain subtle magnetic forces in the earth which tend to pull the energy down. Wool or silk insulates against these forces just as rubber insulates an electrical wire. Traditionally, yogis sit on the skin of a tiger or deer which has died a natural death, but wool or silk works nearly as well. Place the blanket on your chair in such a way that it extends down under your feet and up over the back of your chair.

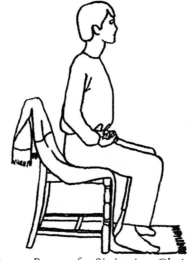

Proper Posture for Sitting in a Chair

Lesson One • Techniques

Proper Posture for Sitting on the Floor

There are several sitting postures that can be used with nearly equal effectiveness. The easiest for most people is a simple cross-legged position using a small cushion. Remember that it is important to keep the spine straight, the chest up and the chin level. In the next section of this course, *The Art and Science of Yoga: 14 Steps to Higher Awareness*, you will learn a number of the sitting poses of *hatha yoga*. For those with good flexibility the lotus pose is traditionally used for meditation, but be sure that whatever pose you use is comfortable. It is much more important to keep your mind fixed on God rather than on the pain in your knees.

Simple Cross-legged Position   The Lotus Pose

Beginning Your Meditation

Always start meditation by completely relaxing the body and mind. Then focus your attention at the point between the eyebrows. This area, called "the spiritual eye," is a center of great spiritual energy. Your eyes should be closed and held steady, and looking slightly upwards, as if looking at a point about an arm's-length away and level with the top of your head.

After you have focused your attention at the point between the eyebrows, feel that you are sending energy there, creating an area of great calmness and peace in the brain. Simply observe your thoughts. Release any thoughts that arise into the vastness of space. Let go of the past and future. You can silently repeat, "I am peaceful, I am peace." As you begin to *feel* the peace of meditation, try to enter into that feeling, deepening it until it pervades your whole being. Feel peace spreading out from your spiritual eye and filling your brain. After some time let it descend, like liquid light, from the brain to enter every cell of your body. Feel that your whole being is made of liquid peace. Hold onto this state for as long as you can, and then gradually feel that you are once again becoming focused at the point between the eyebrows. Try to maintain a sense of deep peace as you end your meditation and resume your daily activities. Feel that your very ability to move and to speak arises out of this inward state.

Routine

It is very important that you establish a daily routine of meditation. As you progress through these lessons you will have a more complete routine to follow. For now your routine is:

- Sit to meditate.

- Check to see that your posture is correct.

- Relax the body completely.

- Concentrate at the point between the eyebrows.

- Offer a prayer for guidance and success in your meditation.

- Feel a deep sense of peace at the point between the eyebrows; let this peace spread into the brain and then throughout the body.

- Hold onto this peace as you resume your activities, or, if it is an evening meditation, as you drift off to sleep.

Do This Today

1. Decide what times of the day you will meditate—probably after awakening in the morning and before bed at night.

2. Decide where you will meditate.

3. Set aside a chair or cushion to sit on.

4. Meditate at the time and in the place you have chosen.

5. Let your first few meditations be guided by using the Companion Audio Disc, tracks 1, 2, and 3.

Resources to Take You Further

Meditation for Starters, by Swami Kriyananda
How to Meditate, by Jyotish Novak
Awaken to Superconsciousness, by Swami Kriyananda

Note: Unless otherwise stated, all recommended resources are available from **Crystal Clarity Publishers**.

See *Further Explorations* section of this book for further information on titles available from Crystal Clarity Publishers.

And visit us on our website: **www.crystalclarity.com**

LEARNING TO RELAX

Lesson 2

Principles

You Need Deep Relaxation to Meditate

A visual image may help you understand the process of deep relaxation. Imagine that you can see the energy patterns of the body. Muscles are luminescent, brightening when they contract and dimming as they relax. Every cell glows as it carries on its tasks. The heart flashes each time it beats, and organs shine brightly as they perform their various functions. You can see which muscles are tense by looking for "hot spots."

The brain and nervous system are especially bright, and you can see constantly shifting waves of energy. A channel of light leads to the brain from each of the sense organs, especially the eyes and ears. Small flashes appear in the brain as information is received and processed, as decisions are made, and signals sent to various parts of the body. The spinal cord is nearly as bright as the brain, glowing as signals go back and forth to every area of the body. You can see circuits in the brain flashing over and over again as the brain thinks, as it remembers, and as it makes decisions.

Look at someone who is asleep. His body is relaxed and appears dim. The heart and respiratory system have slowed down but still flash as they feed the slumbering body. The senses have largely shut down, and their connection with the brain is only a dull glow. The brain itself is surprisingly active, but the patterns are different from those during the waking hours. Most of the sleeping person's energy is centered in the spine and brain.

Now observe someone in deep meditation. In many ways he seems similar to a person who is asleep. The yogi's body is completely relaxed, perhaps even more so than that of a person sleeping. His senses, too, are shut down, but other parts are aglow. Energy has been completely withdrawn into the spine and forepart of the brain. A great master of yoga can withdraw his energy so completely that even the heart and autonomic nervous system are shut down. He has the ability to consciously bring all his energy into a laser-like focus which energizes the spiritual eye, uplifts his consciousness, and eventually raises him to the state of Self-realization.

The first step toward this profound state is relaxation. Relaxation is a result of withdrawing tension and energy from any area, a process normally only partly under our command. But for deep meditation we must learn deep relaxation, which requires conscious control of life-force. Later in this lesson we will learn a technique to completely relax the body, which gets us over the first big hurdle in meditation: physical tension. Keeping your body relaxed and motionless while you are meditating is the first step toward more profound states of consciousness.

Next we must relax the mind, because the biggest challenge is overcoming mental restlessness. When you try to meditate, you will find that your mind wanders, not *because* you are meditating, but simply because you are now quiet enough to finally see how the mind constantly skips from thought to thought in a free-association wonderland. The way to overcome mental restlessness is through concentration. There are a number of extremely effective yogic techniques to improve concentration. Among the most effective are techniques which work with the breath.

One of yoga's great gifts to mankind is the discovery of the link that exists between energy, breath, and mind. As you change one, you also change the other two. If you excite one, the other two become excited and, conversely, if you calm one, the other two respond by becoming calm also. You will notice that if your mind becomes excited, from a sudden fright perhaps, your breath will also speed up. You might also notice that your muscles fill with energy in preparation for action. Observe yourself going through changes in this mind/breath/energy cycle the next time you see a film which plays on your emotions.

The breath is the most outward and, therefore, the easiest of these three linked elements to control. Control your breath and see how quickly it influences your thoughts. This is true in any situation, not just in meditation. A student of these teachings who was in charge of training for the San Francisco Police Department told his rookies that if they wanted to take control of a potentially dangerous confrontation, they had to learn to control themselves first. In order to help them achieve self-control, he taught them to monitor their breathing, to take slow deep breaths. They found it amazingly effective. Try it yourself the next time you are in a tense situation.

Control of the breath and breathing is central to yoga practice. During this course we will learn a number of techniques of breath-control, or *pranayama* as it is called in Sanskrit. Here are several simple but very effective techniques to help you become relaxed and calm for meditation.

Techniques

Techniques for Relaxing the Body

These techniques will help you relax the body. We teach them here as a preparation for meditation, but they can be used any time. They take only a few minutes.

Full Yogic Breath

This technique relaxes the spine and helps to increase and harmonize the energy in the body. It also oxygenates the brain.

Stand erect with feet slightly apart and hands at your sides. Concentrate first on standing with proper posture—spine straight, chest up, and chin level with the floor—the same posture you learned for meditation in the last lesson. Close your eyes and feel that you are centered in your spine. Now, without any strain, bend over as far as is comfortable, exhaling slowly as you do so. By the time the hands have reached the floor you should have exhaled all the air in the lungs. Let the hands rest on your ankles or, if you are flexible enough, touch the floor. Rest in this position for a few moments.

Now begin to inhale and come up gradually until you are fully erect. Bring your hands up slowly as you rise and extend them up over your head. Rise up on your toes as you complete this upward movement. You should inhale slowly during the whole rising motion, filling your lungs completely by the time your arms are above your head. Now, finish the movement by exhaling slowly and once again bringing the hands to the sides. Repeat this movement three to five times, trying to

Steps in the Full Yogic Breath

breathe more and more deeply each time. When you finish, stand erect for a minute or two with your eyes closed. Feel that your body is completely relaxed and filled with energy.

In order to do the full yogic breath correctly you need to breathe very deeply. Begin the inhalation, as you rise, by breathing with your diaphragm (diaphragmatic breathing is taught next). Then, as you rise farther, inhale more deeply, feeling the sides of your chest and rib cage expanding and filling the middle part of your lungs with air. Finally, as you stretch up, fill the upper part of the lungs. Feel that you are filling not only your lungs, but your whole body with air and vitality.

Diaphragmatic Breathing

It is important to learn how to breathe correctly, and this means diaphragmatic breathing. The diaphragm is a dome-shaped muscle between the lungs and the abdominal cavity. As we inhale, it contracts and flattens its curve, creating a vacuum into which the lungs can expand. As this happens the diaphragm pushes the abdominal muscles outward. Watch the stomach of a baby rise and fall as it breathes and you will see this natural process in action. Many adults, however, because of tension, illness, or the desire to have a thin waist, resist this natural movement and have to re-learn it.

Diaphragmatic breathing can, and should, be done in any position, but it is easiest to re-learn when you are most relaxed, lying on the floor. Lie on your back with your arms at your sides, palms upward. Many people find it easier to relax the diaphragm if they bend their knees, placing their feet flat on the floor. Relax completely, especially the stomach and abdomen. Now, breath deeply and slowly, concentrating on the diaphragm, and feeling your stomach rise as you inhale and fall as you exhale. Relax the abdominal muscles more and more

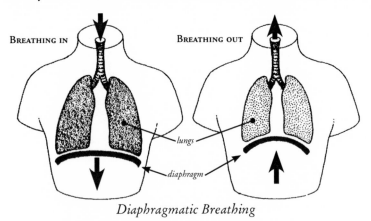

Diaphragmatic Breathing

completely, using the diaphragm, and not the stomach muscles, to create the rise and fall of the abdomen.

After several minutes of practice on the floor you can sit in a cross-legged position and continue diaphragmatic breathing. You may find this a little harder at first but you'll soon catch on. It helps to close your eyes and concentrate on relaxing the stomach, allowing it to swell outward and relax back inward. Once you know how to breathe correctly you can practice diaphragmatic breathing wherever you are. It may take a couple of weeks to re-train yourself but you will find the results well worth the effort. Be sure to check to see that you are breathing diaphragmatically as you begin your meditations.

Poses to Stretch and Relax the Spine

It is very helpful for both meditation and overall health to increase flexibility in the spine. Here are two simple stretches to accomplish that goal. But first, a couple of cautions: 1) Never push past your comfort level when doing any stretch. Always *relax* into a pose, never force yourself. 2) Never hold a posture longer than is comfortable. A few seconds to a minute is sufficient to start with.

A wide variety of yoga postures are taught in detail in the next section of this course, *The Art and Science of Yoga: 14 Steps to Higher Awareness,* which goes much more deeply into the study of *hatha yoga.* But for now, here are some very simple stretches to help relax you in preparation for meditation. They will stretch the spine, helping to relax and energize you for meditation.

The Cobra Pose—A Simple Backward Stretch

Lie face downward, with your palms on the floor next to your shoulders and your forehead resting on the floor. Keep the elbows close to the body. Now slowly raise your head and feel the tension in the back of the neck. Continue to draw the head backward as far as you can using the back and neck muscles alone. Now use your arms to push yourself upward, letting your spine stretch and bend backward. Feel the stretch, and the resulting release of energy, moving from the head downward to the base of the spine. Stretch backward as far as is comfortable, keeping your navel on the floor. Relax as completely as possible, holding this position for a few seconds (or more if it is completely comfortable). Now slowly lower the forehead back to the floor, feeling a reverse flow of energy up the spine. If there is any strain, do a gentler variation by keeping the elbows on the floor as you stretch up and back. You can repeat this stretch two or three times if you like.

The Child Pose

It is always good to balance a stretch of the spine in one direction with another stretch in the opposite direction. Here is a very gentle forward stretch (a variation of the *Hare Pose*.) Sit on your calves with your legs underneath you. Your right big toe should be over your left big toe. If you feel a strain on your legs you can use a small cushion on top of or under your ankles to relieve the pressure. Now bend forward, exhaling as you do so, until your head touches the floor a few inches in front of your knees. Let your arms rest beside your legs. Hold this position for a few seconds (up to a minute if it is completely comfortable), relaxing completely and breathing normally. Return slowly to an upright position and relax for a minute or so.

The Child Pose-final position

Deep Relaxation

Begin as you did for diaphragmatic breathing, lying on your back with your arms at your sides and your palms facing up. Practice diaphragmatic breathing for a few minutes, relaxing more and more deeply. Pay special attention to releasing all tension in your abdomen, feeling it rise and fall like the tide.

Now relax individual areas of your body as deeply as possible, starting with your feet and working your way up slowly to your head. It helps to feel that the area you are relaxing is filled with space or is full of light. Some people prefer to feel that their body is growing heavy rather than light—experiment to see what works best for you.

Start with your feet. Relax them, letting all tension go. Now, deeply relax your calves, and then gradually move up your legs. Pay particular attention to the back of your knees, a place where many people hold tension. Continue up your body, releasing tension in your thighs, hips, and buttocks. Relax each and every part as deeply as you possibly can. Now continue, letting go of all strain in your abdomen and then your chest and shoulders. People often hold tension in their stomach and shoulders, so relax these areas deeply. Continue on, relaxing your neck, jaw, chin, and tongue. Then relax your cheeks and finally your eyes and eyelids. Remain in this deeply relaxed state for several minutes, occasionally checking your body to see if you can find any spots of tension. Now, sit up, but try to remain as relaxed as possible as you do so.

Tensing and Relaxing

This technique was recommended by Paramhansa Yogananda and will help release subconscious tensions. It is especially valuable for meditation and should be used at the beginning of each session. But you can also use it at the beginning of *deep relaxation* or any time you feel tense. To begin, inhale fully through the nose with a "double breath." A double breath is a short inhalation followed immediately by a long inhalation—huh, hhuuuuhh. When you have inhaled tense the whole body until it vibrates, holding the breath as you do so. Then throw the breath out and relax completely. This exhalation should be with a double breath through both the mouth and the nose. Do this three to six times after you sit to meditate.

Centering the Mind

One of Yogananda's principles, which we explore in more depth later in these lessons, is, "The greater the will, the greater the flow of energy." It is easy to see how this applies on a physical level, but it also applies on a mental level. Mentally, we send or withdraw energy according to where we place our attention.

We create mental tension when our thoughts are restless or worried. Moreover, a tense mind is an ineffective mind.

Focusing the mind is especially important when it comes to meditation—in fact, meditation doesn't begin until we are concentrated. Here is a breathing technique which works to help focus your mind.

Regular Breathing

This technique will regularize and harmonize the breath, which, in turn, will produce the same result for your mind. Inhale slowly, counting to eight. Hold the breath for the same eight count while concentrating your attention at the point between the eyebrows. Now exhale slowly to the same count of eight. This is one round of "regular breathing." Depending upon your capacity, you can go more slowly, counting mentally to twelve (inhale to count of twelve, hold for twelve, exhale to count of twelve) or use sixteen count. It is essential, however, that the inhalation, holding, and exhalation be of equal length. Generally speaking, slower is better, but don't go so slowly that you get out of breath. That would be counterproductive. As you do this technique feel that you are becoming increasingly relaxed and focused.

Listening and Focusing

You will greatly reduce your level of mental restlessness simply by becoming more centered in the here and now. One of the most effective ways to do this is through increasingly sensitive listening. First listen to your outer environment. (You won't want to do this in every meditation, but an occasional practice is very helpful.) Try to see how many different sounds you can hear. Start with those that are loudest—sounds in your house or the sounds of traffic. Then try to listen for more subtle sounds such as distant bird songs or wind in the trees. Then become aware of very soft sounds—the sound of your breath or even your heartbeat.

Now start "listening" to your thoughts. Just observe your stream of consciousness. Be careful to maintain the perspective of an observer or listener. Don't get drawn into a thought so completely that you become lost in it. If this happens (and it almost surely will) just bring your attention back to a state of mindfulness. You will probably be quite surprised to see how many thoughts vie for your attention.

Now try to get behind your thoughts and observe your feelings. As you become more still you will see that thoughts often rise out of an underlying emotion: anxiety or concern, hope or fear, love and compassion. Observe these underlying feelings but don't identify with them. Simply become increasingly aware of the play of your consciousness.

Keep your mind focused completely in the present. Let go of the past—of memories, of regrets, of the tendency to think "if only I could change that experience." Simply accept what has happened since it can't be changed anyway. Let go also of thoughts of the future. Don't allow your mind to think about plans or projects. Observe your underlying feelings about the future. Let go of expectations and the anxiety that inevitably accompanies them. Be completely in the "here and now."

As you get more and more interiorized you will become aware of certain fundamental traits of your consciousness. You will feel the deep peace which accompanies inner silence. You will feel an expansive love that radiates out to the whole world.

And you will discover a sense of joy that is not dependent on any circumstances: It simply IS. Meditate on these qualities. Feel them expanding until they fill your consciousness, driving away any tendency of the mind to be restless. Become absorbed in the inner silence!

Routine

Add the new techniques you have learned to your daily routine.

Routine before Meditation

- Full Yogic Breath
- Diaphragmatic Breathing
- Forward and Backward Stretch
- Deep Relaxation

Routine for Meditation

- Pray for guidance.
- Tense and relax with double breath, three to six times.
- Regular breathing, six to twelve rounds
- Deep relaxation of body parts (in sitting position)
- Careful listening
- Absorption in inner silence

Do This Today

1. Work with guided relaxation on the Companion Audio Disc, track 1.
2. Meditate using the new breathing techniques you have learned.
3. Review your daily meditation schedule and make any appropriate changes.

Resources to Take You Further

Ananda Yoga for Higher Awareness, by Swami Kriyananda

Yoga for Busy People, DVD by Gyandev McCord and Lisa Powers

Yoga to Awaken the Chakras, DVD by Gyandev McCord

Yoga for Emotional Health, DVD by Lisa Powers

INTERIORIZATION

Lesson 3

Principles

Using Concentration to Focus Our Minds

Meditation is a journey to the center of your inner self—a journey which can only begin when you withdraw your attention from the outer world. Two things are required in order to make progress: relaxation and concentration. By deep relaxation we are able not only to keep the body still for meditation, but we are also much less disturbed by a multitude of tiny messages from the body which keep the mind restless. As you progress in your meditation practice, you will find that mental restlessness is your main enemy. The only way to defeat it is through concentration. In the last lesson we focused on relaxation. In this lesson we will discuss concentration.

Concentration focuses the power of the mind in much the same way a magnifying glass brings the rays of the sun to a single point. But the mind, unlike a lens, is not passive. It takes an act of will to exclude every scattered thought and focus the mind completely.

The ability to concentrate is an inherent part of human nature, built into our very structure. To succeed in anything, whether in business, sports, or academics, we must be able to concentrate deeply on the task at hand. It is said that when Einstein was concentrating on a problem, he would even forget to eat—occasionally for days at a time! We, too, are bound to achieve victory in our endeavors if we can rivet our attention on the task at hand.

Even though it is such a basic component of success, we are rarely taught *how* to concentrate. In this lesson we will learn the *Hong-Sau* technique, which Paramhansa Yogananda called "the highest technique of concentration." The *Hong-Sau* technique is scientific in its approach, working with fundamental forces of human physiology. We have already discussed briefly how breath, energy, and mind are linked, but now it is time to consider it in greater depth.

We know intuitively that there is a connection between our breath and our ability to concentrate. Notice how you instinctively hold your breath when trying to perform a delicate task such as threading a needle. On the other hand, when our mind and energy are already calm and focused, we can observe that our breath is also calm. The next time you are engrossed in reading a book or listening to music, notice how slow and steady your breath is.

The science of yoga has long recognized that breathing exercises can exert a powerful influence on the mind. In fact, there are a wide variety of breathing techniques called *pranayama*, literally "control of subtle energy." Some teachers limit themselves to the physical aspect of *pranayama*, but there is a much deeper significance.

Breathing techniques work on several levels: On a physical level they help to decarbonize and oxygenate the blood, allowing the respiration to slow down. On a mental level, they give us a simple object on which to focus the mind. Calming the breath also calms our emotions. But, most importantly, breathing techniques allow us to influence the flow of life-force in the body and mind. The reason yoga techniques are so powerful is that they give us a means to control this subtle energy, called *prana* in Sanskrit. *Prana* is finer than the electromagnetic forces of this physical universe. It is the primordial sea of energy from which the very atoms emerge.

No measuring device has yet been able to detect this energy, yet those who have keenly developed awareness can perceive it. People who can see auras are seeing the emanations of the *pranic* or "astral" body. This *prana* (or chi, or ki in other traditions) infuses and sustains the entire material world, and all matter is sustained by it. All life exists because of *prana*.

Yogananda used the term "life-force" to refer to this energy when it manifests itself in living beings, and taught that it is life-force that animates us. Without it we would be inert matter. Christ was referring to this universal life-force when he was tempted by the devil after fasting for forty days in the wilderness and said, "It is written, Man shall not live by bread alone, but by every word that proceedeth out of the mouth of God." (Matthew 4:4) "Word," as used here, means vibration or energy.

It is actually *prana* which sustains the body rather than food, water, and oxygen. Food *seems* necessary to life only because it is a source of condensed *prana*. Occasionally there is a rare individual who is able to bypass the supermarket and live by subtle energy alone. Yogananda writes about two such people in his spiritual classic, *Autobiography of a Yogi*. These two, Therese Neumann from Bavaria and Giri Bala from India, lived their entire adult lives without eating.

As a young girl, Giri Bala had been teased about her insatiable appetite. This roused in her intense determination never to eat again. That day, her guru materialized before her. "Dear little one," he said in a voice of loving compassion, "I am the guru sent here by God to fulfill your urgent prayer. He was deeply touched by its very unusual nature. From today you shall live by the astral light, your bodily atoms fed from the infinite current."

Prana is too subtle for most people to perceive. But, because it is directly connected to the breath, we exert an indirect influence on the *prana* by controlling our inhalation and exhalation, which is relatively easy to do.

Therese Neumann, the famous Catholic stigmatist, spent her entire adult life without food. She took only a small communion wafer during her daily mass. She was frequently tested by medical doctors who verified the apparent "miracle."

The technique you will learn in this lesson, *Hong-Sau*, involves a breathing exercise. Its purpose is not to free us from food, but rather to free us from restless thoughts. Its ultimate purpose is to allow us to become completely internalized. In fact, practiced correctly, it will allow us to achieve 100% concentration. Only then can we experience the deepest states in meditation, and feel our unity with God.

Deep meditation comes spontaneously when our whole being is internalized and focused at the point between the eyebrows (the spiritual eye, or Christ center). This is the seat of concentration, and *Hong-Sau* works with breath, attention, and mantra to focalize all life-force at this center.

The sounds used in this technique, *Hong* (rhymes with "song") and *Sau* (sounds like "saw"), are a *mantra*. A *mantra* is a sound formula which has a certain power. In some cases the *mantra* produces healing or strength or devotion. The special effect of *Hong-Sau*, however, is to calm and internalize our *prana*.

Techniques

Introduction to the Hong-Sau Technique

This technique is relatively simple but extremely important for meditation. From this point on you should practice *Hong-Sau* during every meditation. It is best to practice it near the beginning of your session, immediately after you have relaxed the body and done a few rounds of regular breathing to relax the mind.

Begin by inhaling and then exhaling completely. As the next breath comes in, mentally chant *Hong*. Then, as you exhale, mentally chant *Sau*. Make no attempt to control the breath, just let its flow be completely natural. You should feel that the breath itself is silently making the sounds of *Hong* and *Sau*. In the first phase of the technique, feel the breath at the point where it enters the nostrils. Be as attentive as possible. It will help to bring the forefinger of your right hand slightly toward the palm as you inhale and relax it back as you exhale. If you have difficulty feeling the breath, you can concentrate, for a while, on the breathing process itself, feeling your diaphragm and chest expanding and contracting.

Gradually, as you become more calm, try to feel the breath higher and higher in the nose. Be sure that your gaze is kept steady at the point between the eyebrows throughout your meditation. Don't allow your eyes to follow the movement of the breath. Continue to relax and concentrate more deeply until you can feel the breath high in the nasal cavity. You can then feel that it is awakening and energizing the Christ center at the point between the eyebrows. If you find that your mind has wandered, simply bring it back to an awareness of the breath and the mantra.

At no time during the practice of this technique should you make any effort whatsoever to control the breath. Let it flow naturally. Gradually, you may notice that the pauses between inhalation and exhalation are becoming longer. Enjoy these spaces as a natural result of calmness. You can increase your interiorization by feeling that you are becoming the breath itself and that you are expanding into endless space at the spiritual eye.

As you grow very calm you may notice that the breath is becoming so shallow (or the pauses so prolonged) that it hardly seems necessary to breathe at all. Try to increase this feeling and the sense of complete freedom that accompanies it. In the deepest practice of *Hong-Sau*, energy becomes so internalized that the body goes into a state of suspended animation and the breath stops altogether. But don't try to achieve this state through any act of will. Simply accept it gratefully and joyfully if it comes.

Start by practicing *Hong-Sau* for five to ten minutes at a time. If you are meditating for more than twenty minutes at a sitting, you can practice *Hong-Sau* for up to one half of your meditation time. End your practice of the technique by taking a deep breath, and exhaling three times. Then, keeping your mind focused and your energy completely internalized, try to feel God within as peace, love, or joy.

The amount of time you practice this technique is entirely up to you. But, general speaking, progress in meditation is determined by a combination of intensity of effort and amount of time spent. A few minutes of *Hong-Sau* is unlikely to take you into deep states, although it should help to calm and concentrate your mind. If you want to achieve greater results you will need to increase both the time you spend doing *Hong-Sau* and the total time of your meditations.

Paramhansa Yogananda said that if one wants to become a master of yoga in this life he should practice *Hong-Sau* for at least two hours a day. Yogananda himself, while still a boy, used to practice it for eight hours at a sitting. But you must judge for yourself how much time you feel you can dedicate to your meditations. Don't artificially increase the time past your capacity to enjoy. Meditation is meant to bring you satisfaction and joy.

We are blessed by the energy that flows through us. Try always to end your meditations by praying for those you love and for the world in general.

Routine

Do one or more of the techniques to relax the body before sitting to meditate.

Routine for Meditation

- Pray for grace and guidance.
- Tense and relax (with double breath) three to six times.
- Practice regular breathing for six to twelve rounds.
- Check your posture, then do "deep relaxation" of the individual parts of the body.
- Practice *Hong-Sau* for at least ten minutes or up to one half of your meditation time.
- Stay as long as possible in the inner silence.
- End with a prayer for the world and for your loved ones.

Do This Today

1. Meditate using the Companion Audio Disc, track 4, Guided *Hong-Sau* Meditation.

2. Review your meditation practice to see if you need to make any changes.

Resources to Take You Further

Autobiography of a Yogi, by Paramhansa Yogananda

The New Path: My Life with Paramhansa Yogananda, by Swami Kriyananda

Focusing the Mind: Visualization, Prayer, and Chanting

Lesson 4

Principles

Taking Control

The mind, and its physical instrument, the brain, are restless and must be brought under control before we can meditate properly. In normal waking consciousness, we are programmed to deal with millions of bits of information coming through the senses. After receiving data, we must evaluate it and make countless decisions, most of them completely below the level of conscious awareness.

Think for a moment about the simple act of walking across your living room to soothe a crying baby. Visually you must see your environment so you can walk through it. This involves not just perceiving objects but also continuously evaluating what your eyes are seeing. Another part of your brain is furiously processing feedback from nerves and muscles, allowing you to remain upright, but not so upright that you can't continue the process of controlled falling that we call walking. Your auditory system is handling sounds, yet you are probably not aware of any of these activities. Your mind is thinking simply, "Oh, the poor thing! I wonder why he's crying?"

Is it any wonder that we have a hard time getting this supremely dynamic mind of ours focused when we try to meditate? In this lesson we will learn three powerful techniques to help us: visualization, prayer, and chanting. While it is true that these techniques focus our thoughts, they do much more than this. They connect us directly to Spirit. They are the heart and substance of the religious practices of virtually every spiritual path in the world.

Mental activity might be said to be the defining activity of all the more advanced animals, and this is especially true for mankind. Traditionally, yoga identifies four basic mental processes, which in Sanskrit are called *mon, buddhi, ahankara*, and *chitta. Mon* (the mind) is the act of receiving information. Next comes *buddhi* (the intellect), where we process, recognize, and relate the information to pre-existing knowledge, often giving it a name. Then with *ahankara* (the ego) we evaluate it according to how it affects us. Finally, through *chitta* (the feelings) we judge it positively or negatively according to our feelings and our learned likes and dislikes. Yogananda emphasized the feeling aspect of *chitta*, but it is occasionally translated as "mind stuff" and used to define the whole mental process.

Initially comes *mon*, the mind, which is responsible for receiving information. We take in an endless stream of input from the senses. The sense organs are designed to translate energy in the form of waves, pressures, or chemicals into electrical signals. These signals are sent, by an electrochemical process, to the appropriate part of the brain. This is an amazingly complex operation—the visual cortex of the brain alone is made up of billions of neurons! Yet, even though we have received the input, we haven't yet made sense out of it any more than a mirror recognizes images reflected in its surface.

Once the brain receives the raw data from the senses we must then process it into a coherent perception of the world. This "processing," the action of *buddhi*, is an even greater source of mental activity than the reception itself. Modern research shows that sight, for instance, relies on extremely complex interactions between different parts of the brain. We construct a series of overlapping "maps" using highly specialized regions of the cerebral cortex. Some nerve cells "see" only straight vertical lines, others see only straight horizontal lines, or curves, or movement, or color. All of these maps, at least a dozen, must be somehow coordinated and combined into a consistent whole in order for us to see and then to recognize a puppy, a pencil, or a parent.

After processing all this basically neutral information we then personalize it and relate it to ourselves through *ahamkara*, the ego principle. We continually (but subconsciously) ask, "Is this mine or not mine? How does it affect me? Will this be positive or negative for me—for my body, my territory, my family, my possessions, my opinions? Does this threaten me in any way?" Quiet your mind sufficiently to observe your thoughts and you will see that the majority of mental agitation is caused by concerns about your ego.

Yet, evaluating things as to whether they affect our ego does not necessarily bind us to delusion. Even saints, after all, must take care of their bodies. Through the influence of *chitta*, however, we judge the world according to our likes and dislikes. It is this, above all, that keeps us enslaved in the dream world of matter. The heart's energy becomes involved and we create an endless stream of desires and repulsions. While we are usually unaware of our constant judgments, they determine our level of happiness more than anything else. They determine whether the world pleases or disappoints us. If in meditation you can pull back from your likes and dislikes and simply observe your mind, you will quickly be able to focus your energy. In fact,

Patanjali, an ancient and universally respected sage, gave as his classic definition of yoga, *"Yogas chitta vritti nirodh"* — "Yoga is the neutralization of the vortices of likes and dislikes." The blissful state of union with God waits in the silent calmness just beyond our likes and dislikes.

How do we still the mind and emotions? *By deeply focusing our energy and thoughts.* In the last lesson we learned a very powerful technique, *Hong-Sau,* for concentrating our energy. Calming the energy will automatically calm the thoughts and feelings.

One of the great benefits of yoga is that it recognizes everything simply as different levels of energy. It doesn't judge things as good or evil but rather evaluates actions and decisions according to their ability to increase or decrease energy. Through experience we learn that we are inherently more happy when our energy expands and increasingly unhappy as it contracts. Unlike some religious dogmas, yoga doesn't try to suppress energy, but gives us techniques to channel it, ways to transmute thoughts rather than repress them.

In meditation we strive to achieve a state of consciousness in which the mind is calm, focused, and expansive. But to succeed we must first escape the tendency toward restlessness. Visualization, prayer, and chanting each help to focus our minds and direct them toward Spirit. Each works with a different function of the mind, and each, if done correctly, has the power to connect us directly to our own higher self, the superconsciousness. These three activities, present in all religions, are the primary practices of most spiritual paths.

Techniques

Visualization

Visualization is easy to do, but there are a few principles to keep in mind in order to practice it effectively. Concentrate in the forehead and imagine the scene as if it were being shown on a screen. Try to see the image in as great a detail as possible: The more clearly you visualize something the more powerful will be its effect. See it in vibrant color and clear detail.

A visualization should be both beautiful and expansive, since its purpose is to uplift the mind as well as focus it. Involve more senses than just sight. If you are visualizing a lake, *hear* the wavelets lapping on the shore, *feel* the breeze blowing over the water, even *smell* the wildflowers on the banks. Above all, immerse yourself in the scene to the exclusion of all other thoughts.

There are many types of visualization but three kinds are especially helpful for meditation. The first one helps calm and focus the mind, the second expands our consciousness, and the third attunes us to a saint or spiritual guide.

Here's an example of a calming and focusing visualization: Imagine a meadow filled with tall grass and flowers. The sun shines brightly and a gentle breeze is blowing, stirring everything into motion, swaying the plants back and forth. You can hear the sound of crickets and smell the gentle aroma of the flowers. Gradually, the breezes cease and the meadow becomes calm. All movement stops, everything becomes completely still, as if waiting. Your thoughts, like the grass, become totally still. In this stillness you become aware of an overwhelming sense of peace and well-being. Bathe yourself in this feeling for as long as possible.

A second type of visualization expands our consciousness, allowing it to reach outward to infinity. Visualize a deep blue or golden light in your forehead. When you see it clearly, feel it filling your whole brain. Gradually let it expand to fill your whole body. Feel it infusing and healing every cell. This light is conscious and has a wisdom of its own. You don't need to direct it, but simply allow it to touch every fiber of your being. Now let this light expand beyond the boundaries of your body. Let it fill the room you are in, bonding you to all others there with you. Feel that the light is energizing every atom it touches, lifting the vibration of every particle of matter. Now let it continue to expand into your town and gradually spread over your state, your country, and then the whole planet. Feel it healing and uplifting everyone and everything that it touches. Now, let the light expand beyond this planet into the solar system and then the galaxy, finally bathing the entire universe in its glow. Float in this vast ocean of light, releasing all sense of separation until you and the light are one.

A third very powerful technique is to visualize a saint or spiritual guide. Here, at Ananda, we regularly visualize Yogananda or one of the others in our guru line. This is a great aid in attuning ourselves with the divine consciousness manifested in someone who has attained the high states that we yearn for. Start by looking at a photo until you have the image clearly in mind. Then, close your eyes and clearly visualize that image. Try, especially, to see the eyes clearly. The eyes are the windows of the soul and, more than any other part of us, help convey consciousness. Magnetically draw the saint's attributes—the wisdom, the love, the joy—into your own consciousness. Know that in your higher self, you and that saint are one.

Prayer

Every religion counsels prayer, but most people are disappointed with the results of their prayers. This is because they are praying in the wrong way. Yogananda gave clear guidelines for effective prayer. First of all, he said that we must pray with our full consciousness—as Jesus said, "with all your heart, with all your mind, with all your soul, and with all your strength." God answers all prayers, but those with little energy behind them He answers only a little. Those with real power elicit a potent response.

Pray believing. Don't let doubts and insecurities block your expectation of success. Assume that God *wants* to answer your prayers (as long as they are for your benefit, not your harm). Pray with the thought that you are God's very own child and not a beggar pleading for favors from a stranger. Beggarly prayers keep God distant, while praying as His son or daughter brings Him close. Don't feel unworthy: Identify with your potential, not your failings. Yogananda said, "The greatest sin is to call yourself a sinner."

Let your prayers be simple and from your heart. Formal prayers create a stiff relationship with God casting Him in the role of someone whom we must please with fancy words and actions before He will accept or love us. But, in reality, He is the nearest of the near and the dearest of the dear. He is closer to us than our own thoughts and loves us more than we can ever love ourselves.

Here is a beautiful and simple prayer from Yogananda's book *Whispers from Eternity*, which you can use as a model for your own prayers. Read it over several times to get in touch with the images and meaning of the words. Then repeat it with closed eyes, going deeply into the feeling behind the words. As you continue to saturate the prayer with your soul feelings, you will spiritualize it, giving it a power far beyond the mere words.

We Demand as Thy Children

Thou art our Father. We are made in Thine own image. We are sons of God. We neither ask nor pray like beggars, but demand as Thy children, wisdom, salvation, health, happiness, eternal joy. Naughty or good, we are Thy children. Help us to find Thy will in us. Teach us to use independently the human will (since Thou gavest that to us to use freely), in tune with Thy wisdom-guided will.

Note: The use of *Thou* and *Thy* may sound somewhat formal to the modern ear, since they are less used now, but it is actually the familial or more intimate form of address in English.

Chanting

Chanting—the repetitive singing of a few words or sentences—is very similar to prayer. In fact, many of the chants that we sing at Ananda are simply prayers set to music. Adding melody and rhythm to a prayer makes it easier to get engaged. In chanting, the same rules apply as in praying: Concentrate deeply, chant with your whole being, and try to get behind the words into the essence of the chant. Yogananda said, "Chanting is half the battle." It is one of the very best ways to open the heart.

At Ananda's centers and churches we chant together at the beginning of nearly every group meditation. Then we carry the chant into the silent part of the meditation, trying to open our hearts more and more completely to God. You can chant silently at any time: while working, or driving, or while otherwise wasting time standing in line. Regular chanting will awaken love and devotion in your heart and keep your meditations from getting dry.

Someone once told Yogananda that Americans had no devotion. Yogananda smiled quietly and asked the man to come that evening to a program he was scheduled to give at Carnegie Hall in New York. At that program he led an audience of several thousand in singing the following chant for nearly two hours! Many, he said, went into a state of ecstasy that night. Others were healed of serious illness.

O GOD BEAUTIFUL

O God beautiful, O God beautiful,
  At Thy feet, oh, I do bow.
O God beautiful, O God beautiful,
  In the forest Thou art green,
  In the mountains Thou art high,
  In the river Thou art restless,
  In the ocean Thou art grave.

O God beautiful, O God beautiful,
  At Thy feet, oh, I do bow.
O God beautiful, O God beautiful,
  To the serviceful Thou art service,
  To the lover Thou art love,
  To the sorrowful Thou art sympathy,
  To the yogi Thou art bliss.

O God beautiful, O God beautiful,
  At Thy feet, oh, I do bow,
O God beautiful, O God beautiful!

Chant is included on the Companion Audio Disc, track 5.

Generally speaking, you should use these three techniques—visualization, prayer, and chanting—toward the beginning of your meditation. You should leave at least one third of your meditation time for going beyond words and inwardly communing with Spirit. These techniques should bring you to a state of deep calmness and focus. As you feel a sense of inwardness, try to increase the feeling by bathing yourself in that inner poise. Don't allow restlessness to creep back into the mind. Stay in the calm inner poise of your soul for as long as you can, letting it infuse your whole being. Even when you are ready to leave your meditation seat, feel that you are carrying a bubble of peace and joy with you. Let your activity spring from that state. Speak from that state. Relate from that state. See how it will transform your life!

Routine

- Do the full yogic breath three times and then a few minutes of diaphragmatic breathing.

Routine for Meditation

- Check to see that your posture is correct.
- Pray for grace and guidance.
- Tense and relax (with double breath) three to six times.
- Practice regular breathing for six to twelve rounds.
- Do deep relaxation from toes to head.
- Relax the mind, setting aside all thoughts of past and future.
- Practice *Hong-Sau* for a few minutes.
- Use one or more of the techniques from this lesson: Chant for several minutes, do a visualization, or repeat a deep prayer many times. Whichever you choose, try to lose yourself in the practice.
- Stay as long as possible in the inner silence.
- End with a prayer for your loved ones and for the world.

Do This Today

At the appropriate time in your meditation, you may wish to use the guided meditation with visualization on the Companion Audio Disc, tracks 1 and 2.

Resources to Take You Further

Meditation for Starters, CD, (a guided meditation and visualization) by Swami Kriyananda

Metaphysical Meditations, CD, by Swami Kriyananda

A wonderful chanting series from Ananda Kirtan, featuring chants by Paramhansa Yogananda and Swami Kriyananda. Titles include:

Bliss Chants
Divine Mother Chants
Power Chants
Peace Chants
Love Chants
Wisdom Chants
Wellness Chants

EXPANSION

Lesson 5

Principles

Superconsciousness

Self-realization does not require an accumulation of intellectual knowledge. Nor do we need to conform to some predetermined standard of behavior. Union with the Infinite comes when we simply remember who we really are. Patanjali, the great sage of yoga, defined union with God as *smriti—*memory. This kind of memory, however, will not be experienced in lower states of consciousness. We must first calm the turbulence of the subconscious and conscious minds. Only then can we get in touch with our central reality, the superconsciousness. In this uplifted state the distorting filters of "mind stuff" drop away and we perceive through pure intuition.

The book *Superconsciousness: A Guide to Meditation* by Swami Kriyananda begins with this paragraph: "Consciousness, in its pure state, is absolute: more absolute than the speed of light, which slows on entering a material medium such as the earth's atmosphere; more absolute than the existence of matter, which is only a manifestation of energy; more absolute than energy, which is itself a vibration of consciousness."

He goes on to say, "One often hears references to 'altered states of consciousness.' Implied in the expression is a suggestion that higher states of awareness are anomalies.

"Actually, there is only one state of consciousness: superconsciousness. The conscious and subconscious minds are our 'altered states,' representing as they do the downward filtering of superconsciousness through the brain. Superconsciousness is, forever, the reality. It is our true and native state of being."

The stages of relaxation and interiorization are necessary preparation for the final stage: expansion of awareness into superconsciousness. In order to experience our true self we must first relax, concentrate, and elevate our energy. Throughout this course, we have used the term "meditation" a little loosely, employing it to characterize the *process* rather than the actual *state* of meditation. Most of the time when we say we are meditating we aren't; we are struggling to quiet the restless mind sufficiently to *be able* to meditate. The actual state of meditation begins when we have deep concentration without a single disrupting thought.

The higher stages of meditation are composed of three increasingly deep steps. In Sanskrit they are called *dharana, dhyana,* and *samadhi,* which translate into English as concentration, meditation, and union. Since this subject is dealt with more completely in the next part of this course, *The Art and Science of Yoga: 14 Steps to Higher Awareness*, here we will only touch on them briefly. *Dharana* is the state of deep, undisturbed concentration. If, for instance, we are seeing a light at the spiritual eye (between the eyebrows) in the stage of *dharana*, we will have no thought other than the perception of light. If we can hold that state of complete concentration long enough we will enter the next stage of meditation, *dhyana*. Here, we would become absorbed in the light, feeling it to be our true reality. We would no longer retain the slight sense of separation needed to be an "observer" of the light. Then, after some time of being absorbed in the light, we would enter the final stage of meditation, *samadhi*. Here, we would realize that we are one with the light, completely losing any egoic sense of "I-ness." Realizing that the "I" we cling to is only light, we would finally become free of all limitation. In *samadhi* we lose all sense of separation. It is this state of *samadhi* which is the goal of meditation. While it is the quest of lifetimes to achieve *samadhi*, we can and should feel a sense of expansion every time we sit to meditate.

Expansion, then, is the third and final stage of meditation. It comes automatically once we have successfully completed the preceding two stages, relaxation and interiorization. Expansion is our true nature, a memory of bliss, waiting patiently for us to withdraw our attention and energy from the world. The techniques that you have learned are the path which leads to this expanded state. Relaxation techniques allow you to quiet your body and mind. *Hong-Sau* allows you to withdraw your *prana* and achieve deep concentration. In the next lesson, *The Energization Exercises*, you will learn another technique which will give you greater control over the flow of *prana* in your body. With life-force control and deep sincere effort, the higher states of meditation finally become possible.

Always spend at least the last third of your meditation trying to feel an expanded sense of self. When the mind becomes still you will feel an inherent peace and joy. This feeling, Yogananda said, is the sign that God is with you. Try very sensitively to deepen this state. Expand your peace or joy until it permeates your entire being. With sincere yearning blow on the little ember of peace until it bursts into flame and consumes any remaining restlessness. From that state will come an inner communion with God. In that state your sympathies will expand instinctively. You will not have to make any effort to love others: You will not be *able* to feel differently. You will feel a deep connection to all life.

Once a saint was taking a bath in the Ganges. A man sitting on the bank watched as a scorpion climbed to the edge of a branch overhanging the river and fell into the water. The saint picked up the poor creature and put it back in its tree, but was stung as he did so. Again the scorpion crawled out and fell into the water, again the saint replaced it, and again was stung. This episode repeated itself yet a third time.

The observer of this scene could contain himself no longer. He called out, "Why do you keep putting the beast back in the tree when your only reward is getting stung?"

"Don't be angry with it. To sting, you see, is the scorpion's nature. It can't help itself," said the saint.

"But *you* know it is going to attack you. Why do you continue to pick it up?" asked the man.

"My nature is to befriend it, and I can't help myself either," replied the saint.

Contact us: course@ananda.org • 530.470.2340

Techniques

Attuning to the Qualities of God

It is said in the Indian Scriptures that God manifests himself as eight basic qualities: light, sound, wisdom, power, calmness, peace, love, and bliss. In meditation, through superconsciousness, we can attune ourselves to these qualities, any one of which can help us experience great expansion of consciousness.

Practice *Hong-Sau* or one of the techniques from the last lesson (visualization, prayer, or chanting) until you have achieved some degree of stillness and concentration. Now, choose one of the qualities mentioned above and feel, very sensitively, for its presence within. We will use peace in the following example. As you perceive some sense of peace, focus all your concentration on deepening the feeling. Allow it to expand by practicing a kind of "relaxed effort." It may help, in the beginning, to use a simple affirmation such as "I feel peaceful, I am peace" to help crystallize the feeling, but gradually try to go beyond words into the feeling itself. As the feeling of peace increases, identify with it. In other words, let peace, rather than your personality, become the way you define yourself. Increase this state as much as possible and hold onto it for as long as you can.

This is the last stage of meditation, and it is not necessary to practice any further techniques at this point. To commune with one of God's qualities is to commune with God Himself, who manifests through these vibrations.

After you have stayed in this wordless vibration of peace for as long as possible you will probably experience the mind beginning to think thoughts once again. Now is a good time to send your blessings out into the world. Visualize peace spreading out from you in ever-expanding circles. Let it touch everything and everyone. Let the whole planet be bathed in your universal peace.

Meditation on the Guru

The various aspects of God mentioned above become fully manifested only in a God-realized soul. A true guru has long since become completely free from any egoic identification, any separation from God. Such a soul incarnates only to help teach and free others. In the third, *Discipleship,* section of the *Ananda Course in Self-realization* we will go into the guru-disciple relationship in depth. But even if you don't yet feel any urge to become the disciple of such a one, it is still helpful to meditate on their consciousness. This can be done in several ways.

It is very beneficial to contemplate the lives and words of a God-realized soul. See the episodes in their lives as models for your own attitudes and behavior. Try to see the meaning *behind* their actions, the teaching implicit in their conduct. The writings of a great soul carry a transforming power within them. One time a disciple told Paramhansa Yogananda how changed he had been by reading his book, *Autobiography of a Yogi.* Yogananda replied, "That is because I put my vibrations into it."

When you meditate on the words or the life story of a guru, feel that he or she is guiding your thoughts, instructing and uplifting you. Commune as deeply as possible. The modern saint Therese Neumann of Bavaria would go into a state of ecstasy every week through the contemplation of Christ's passion. She became so deeply identified with Christ that she expressed in her own body the wounds of the cross—she was what is known as a stigmatist.

As we mentioned in the last lesson, you can also meditate on the guru, visualizing him or her in meditation. Try to magnetically draw the consciousness by looking deeply into the saint's eyes. Feel that you are becoming one.

Longer Rhythms: Long Meditations, Silence, Seclusion, and Retreats

As well as expanding your consciousness through daily meditations, you should also look at the longer rhythms of your life. It is easy to get into a spiritual rut. One way to avoid this is to have at least one long meditation each week. Not only will you find that you can go deeper in a long meditation, but your daily sessions will soon begin to seem short. A good rule of thumb is to have one meditation that is about three times as long as your usual ones. If you are normally meditating for a half hour at a time, try once a week to meditate for one and a half hours. Build up over time to the point where you can comfortably have a long meditation of three hours.

Another practice that will greatly benefit your spiritual evolution is to have a period of silence once a week, or even better, once a day. You will be amazed at how much mental restlessness is caused simply by making noise! Try regularly to spend a few hours, or even a whole day without talking. During this time, avoid watching TV, listening to the radio, and, preferably, listening to music. If you feel, out of force of habit, a need to have background sound, make sure that any music you play is uplifting and God-reminding. Likewise, anything you read during this time should be spiritual.

It is extremely beneficial to have a few days of seclusion once a year. Many have found that this is one of the most important factors in deepening their spiritual life. It is like an extended period of your weekly silence, an opportunity to stay in an uplifted state of consciousness for days at a time. Great insights can come during such a period. After a few days one begins to see old habit patterns in a completely new perspective. One develops a new sense of priorities. Yogananda often said, "Seclusion is the price of greatness." If seclusion is a new concept to you it might be helpful to have a "guided seclusion" for your first experience. At Ananda, we have a *Seclusion Retreat* where guests are welcome and such guidance is available.

Consider also taking a spiritual retreat. It will be an opportunity to spend time with others who share your goals, and a chance to ask questions and get further instruction about your practices. At Ananda we have a meditation retreat called *The Expanding Light* which is open year round. You can choose from a wide variety of classes and programs and spend time with staff members who have been meditating daily for many years. An occasional visit will help reinvigorate your spiritual life. We have included a program guide in the course material.

Routine

- Do a few relaxation exercises.

- Pray for grace and guidance.

- Practice *Hong-Sau* for a few minutes.

- Tune into one of the qualities (peace, joy, love, etc.) of God. Expand into the quality you have chosen.

- Stay as long as possible in this vibration.

- End by projecting this quality to your loved ones and to the world.

Do This Today

1. Pick a convenient time for a long meditation.
2. Choose a time this week when you can practice several hours of silence.
3. Schedule a retreat.

Resources to Take You Further

Superconsciousness: A Guide to Meditation
   by Swami Kriyananda

The Expanding Light (Ananda's guest facility),
   14618 Tyler Foote Road, Nevada City, CA 95959
   800.346.5350
   www.expandinglight.org

Ananda Seclusion Retreat
   14618 Tyler Foote Road, Nevada City, CA 95959
   530.292.3024
   www.meditationretreat.org

ENERGIZATION EXERCISES

Lesson 6

Principles

Learning to Control Your Energy

As we have seen throughout these lessons, energy control is a fundamental part of the science of yoga. We are beings of energy. Matter, in fact, is merely a projection of underlying energy patterns. In this lesson you will learn a technique called the *Energization Exercises*, which will help you control your life-force. It would be hard to overstate the value of these exercises, which were developed by Yogananda specifically to teach us how to gain control over subtle energy *(prana)*. Yogananda said that if we were stranded on a desert island and could have only one yogic technique, we should choose the Energization Exercises, because through them we would eventually discover the entire science of yoga.

As aspiring yogis, we should learn to see our bodies as the outward expression of elemental energy patterns. Our bodies, our health, our happiness, our very thoughts are determined by the level and direction of our energy. We should see our whole life as being like an image on a movie screen, simply patterns of light and dark. We have an enormously powerful tool to change ourselves once we grasp the fact that we are merely projections of energy patterns. If we create the patterns in our lives, then it is possible to *change those patterns directly*. With that realization we have in hand the secret key to the kingdom of God, for, in reality, all that is needed to find God is to release our identification with false images of who we are.

In order to change something, it is much more effective to learn to control energy, which lies behind matter, than to try to control matter itself. Once the pattern has become frozen into its outward manifestation it is much more difficult to change. Isn't it much easier to adjust the *plans* for a house than to move walls around once the house is built?

Consider this example. The introduction of computer modeling has totally transformed the way the aircraft and auto industries design and construct models of new parts. Formerly, once a new part was designed, a highly skilled craftsman had to produce a model out of wood or metal. If minor changes were needed, he had to craft the new part again and again until the new design was perfected. This process was repeated for thousands of parts. Now everything is designed with computer programs that create three-dimensional models on the screen. Parts can be matched to connecting pieces directly in the computer, where everything exists only as patterns of energy. If a physical piece is needed, it is created effortlessly by using light-sensitive plastic and computer controlled lasers. By working with energy patterns rather than physical models, the design time has been cut from years to months.

Scientists are even looking for materials, such as liquid metal, that can be formed directly into the various pieces required. Imagine an auto parts store which could produce, on demand, any part for any model of car ever made. All the necessary information would exist as energy patterns in a computer's memory.

We are not all that different from this example. We, too, exist as dynamic changing projections of underlying energy patterns. If we can learn to control our *prana* and change the underlying patterns sufficiently, we can work miracles for ourselves and others.

Here is just a partial idea of the benefits of being able to control and harmonize the flow of *prana*.

In the Body

We can have boundless energy for work, relationships, and fun. When we become tired, we can recharge the body and mind instantaneously. We can have vibrant good health since the cells in our body would always be highly energized. If we are injured, we can heal the injuries. Does this sound impossible? It wasn't for Jesus or Yogananda or other advanced yogis. Does it mean we will never get ill? Not necessarily, but if we do get ill we can consciously direct sufficient healing energy to allow us to quickly regain our health.

In the Mind

We can easily focus the mind on the task at hand, whether work or meditation. Success is guaranteed because we are able to apply the energy needed to overcome any obstacles in our path. We would have negative moods only rarely, and if they came, we would have a way of dealing with them, since our moods and thoughts are dependent upon our level of energy. We can find it much easier to overcome unwanted attitudes and habits. We can attract to ourselves the people and circumstances that we want: The laws of magnetism are directly related to the laws of energy.

In the Soul

We can find it easy to go into deep meditation and quickly attain stillness of mind and openness of heart. Our devotion can have tremendous power and quickly attract the blessings of God and the masters. Our prayers for others and for the world can be powerful and effective. One time Yogananda and another devotee walked by Rajarshi Janakananda, Yogananda's most advanced disciple, as he was meditating in the garden. As they were passing, Yogananda cautioned the devotee to be very quiet. When they were out of hearing, he said, "You have no idea what blessings are drawn to this work simply by having one person meditate that deeply."

Results like these are possible, but they are not easy to achieve. It all starts by learning to feel and direct the flow of *prana*. Yogananda discovered that, through will power, we can send energy to the various parts of the body. He then made this discovery practical by devising a system of body-cell recharging called the *Energization Exercises*.

Techniques

These exercises are Paramhansa Yogananda's unique contribution to the science of yoga. They use a combination of concentration, will, and breath to direct the flow of energy to various body parts. This flow is sent and withdrawn by tensing and then relaxing the muscles in the area we want to recharge. Paramhansa Yogananda explained that we draw *prana* indirectly through the food we eat, as well as through oxygen and sunlight. These indirect sources of energy, however, are like the water you put into the battery of your car. When the battery runs down, no amount of water will make it work again. You have to recharge the battery from another source. Similarly, Yogananda explained, our bodies live only indirectly from food, but we live directly from the cosmic energy that flows into our bodies through the medulla oblongata at the base of the brain.

The lips and tongue comprise the mouth of *man*, because this is where we eat in a physical way, but the mouth of *God* is the medulla oblongata, inside the hollow point at the base of the skull. This is where we receive the divine energy which truly sustains us. It is from the medulla that we will send energy to various parts of the body by tensing and relaxing the appropriate muscles.

Paramhansa Yogananda gave us the axiom "The greater the will, the greater the flow of energy." Will power should be applied with intensity, but not grimly or with tension. It might help you to think in terms of willingness, enthusiasm, and joy. These Energization Exercises are a means of using will, with awareness of energy, to consciously draw cosmic energy into the body. As you do the movements of the exercises, try to feel the flow of energy and be conscious of that flow. Then, by use of your will power, you can direct the flow of energy to specific parts of the body. The more you become aware of using your will power to direct that energy, the more you will be able to increase the flow.

By way of illustration: Close your eyes and gaze, as in meditation, toward the spiritual eye. Concentrate your attention in the area of the medulla. Now tense your right hand and forearm, feeling that you are sending energy from the medulla to hand and forearm. Continue tensing harder and harder until your hand is vibrating with the effort. Now relax the muscles and feel the energy in the area you have just tensed.

At first what you'll feel is just the tension inside of the muscles. Then you'll experience the flow of energy which creates the tension in those muscles. Finally, you will become aware of how you can direct that flow. It may help to visualize a flow of light. It is important, however, to try to *feel* the flow of energy. It is essential to concentrate as deeply as possible. Now repeat the same thing on the other side, tensing, and then relaxing, the left hand and forearm.

Key Points for Practicing the Energization Exercises

I. **CONCENTRATE ON THE FLOW OF ENERGY.** Before beginning the Energization Exercises, visualize energy coming into the body through the medulla oblongata (located in the indentation, at the base of the skull) and flowing through the body. Once you've learned the exercises, try to keep your eyes closed with your gaze upward toward the point between the eyebrows. This will help you to interiorize your consciousness and draw more on the superconscious. As you do the exercises, first concentrate on the center of the body part(s) that you are tensing and relaxing. Then, as you go deeper, your concentration should be *more on the flow of the energy.*

2. USE CONSCIOUS WILL AS YOU DO THE EXERCISES. Through the use of your will, direct energy to flow into the appropriate body parts to energize the cells. Feel that, through the agency of your will, you are consciously drawing and directing the limitless stream of energy into your body. After tensing an area, completely relax and feel the results. Conscious relaxation after each exercise is very important. Tensing and relaxing not only recharges the body with energy but, even more importantly, trains us to bring the flow of *prana* under our control.

3. REMEMBER YOGANANDA'S AXIOM: "THE GREATER THE WILL, THE GREATER THE FLOW OF ENERGY." This is a spiritual law. While it is better to think of will as "willingness" in order to avoid making it seem grim, you should use your will very intensely, especially during the tensing parts of the exercise. Remember: "Tense with will—relax and feel."

4. TENSE GRADUALLY, AND RELAX GRADUALLY—FROM LOW TO MEDIUM TO HIGH TENSION. Never tense quickly, jerkily, or so hard that you cause physical discomfort. You don't want to "strip your muscle gears." Tense in a continuous wave—low, then medium, and then high with maximum tension, until the muscles vibrate. Hold the tension for three to four seconds.

After tensing, relax completely—from high, to medium, to low, and finally to no tension.

5. PRACTICE THE EXERCISES WITH "DOUBLE BREATHING."
Most of the Energization Exercises call for double breathing. Double breathing is a short and long inhalation through the nose and a short and long exhalation through the nose and mouth. This double breath allows you to inhale and exhale more deeply and to oxygenate the blood. To practice a "double breath," begin by inhaling strongly through the nose with a short, sharp inhalation followed directly by a long, strong inhalation—completely filling your lungs. Then, without pause, exhale twice through the nose and mouth with a short, then a long exhalation—making the sound: "Huh, Huhhhhhh." Feel cosmic energy flowing into the medulla oblongata with the breath.

6. IT IS BEST TO PRACTICE THE EXERCISES OUTDOORS.
If you are unable to do this make sure you do them in front of an open window or door where fresh air can enter.

7. PRACTICE THE EXERCISES EVERY DAY AT LEAST ONCE, AND PREFERABLY TWICE A DAY.
Each exercise should be done from three to five times. Once you have learned all the exercises it should take ten-fifteen minutes to do them. Energization can be practiced before meditation to release tensions and allow you to go deeper and sit more still in meditation, or at any time.

8. MODIFY IF NECESSARY.
If you have back, neck or any special physical problems or if a body part is ill or injured, modify the exercises for these body parts or practice the exercises for these areas mentally or with low tension only. It

may be helpful to visualize a current of light flowing to the affected part.

9. ISOLATE THE BODY PART BEING TENSED. If you cannot isolate a specific muscle or body part, put your mind there and the energy will automatically flow to that part. Later you may be able to actively locate and tense the muscles there individually.

10. TRY TO DO ALL THE EXERCISES. While you are learning them, you can begin by learning and practicing a few of the exercises at a time until you've worked up to doing them all each day. You might try practicing the first five or so exercises for a week, then adding more the next week, and so on. There are visual and audio aids that you can use to help learn the exercises more quickly—the *Ananda Energization Exercises* DVD, the *Energization Exercises* CD, and our *Energization Poster*.

11. DO THE EXERCISES WITH JOY AND WILLINGNESS. Feel that you are giving your body a "breakfast of energy". You may want to keep this affirmation in mind as you practice: *Within me lies the energy to accomplish all that I will to do. Behind my every act is God's infinite power.*

The Energization Exercises

Do each exercise three to five times
unless otherwise indicated. If an exercise
alternates between both sides of the body
always start first on the left side.

Begin with this prayer:

"O, Infinite Spirit,
   recharge my body with Thy Cosmic Energy,
   my mind with Thy concentration,
   my soul with Thy ever-new joy.
O, eternal youth of body and mind,
   abide in me forever and forever."

1. Double Breathing *(with palms touching)*

With your arms straight out to your sides at shoulder level,
double exhale as you bring your palms
together in front, bending the knees slightly. Double inhale as you straighten up and
bring your arms back out, with hands as
fists, tensing the entire body in an upward
wave. Double exhale as you relax in a
downward wave.

Do this three to five times.

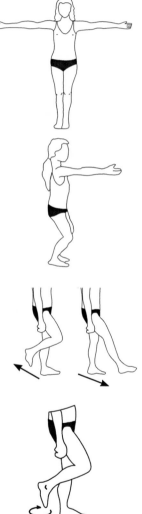

2. Calf Recharging

Standing on your right foot, slowly bend
your left knee, bringing your foot up behind
while tensing your calf muscle. Relax tension at the top, then tense the calf again as
you bring your foot back down.

*Do this three times with your left leg, then do
ankle rotation (see next exercise).*
Then repeat three times on the right.

3. Ankle Rotation

Rotate the ankle in small circles, with tension around the ankle.

Do this three times in each direction.
(Do this after calf recharging on each side.)

4. Calf-Forearm/Thigh-Upper Arm

Place your left foot forward, with most of your weight on the right foot. Tense your left calf and left forearm together with low, medium, and then high tension. Relax. Then tense your left thigh and upper arm together.

Do this sequence three times on the left, then three times on the right.

Then with your weight on both legs equally, tense both calves and both forearms simultaneously. Relax, and tense both thighs and both upper arms.

Do this sequence three times, also.

5. Chest and Buttock Recharging

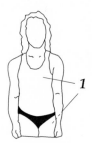

Simultaneously tense your left buttock muscles and the left side of your chest, then relax.

Repeat on the right side. Do this three times.

6. Back Recharging

Tense the muscles of your **lower left back** (just at the waist), then relax.

Repeat on the right side. Alternate sides, tensing, and relaxing each three times.

Then tense the muscles of your **middle back**, the area around the shoulder blades.

Repeat on the right side. Alternate sides, tensing, and relaxing each three times.

Then tense the muscles of your **upper back**, just above the shoulder blades.

Repeat on the right side. Alternate sides, tensing, and relaxing each three times.

7. Shoulder Rotation

With your fingertips resting on your shoulders, rotate your arms and shoulders in large circles, with tension in the shoulders. Be sure to move your shoulders, not just your arms.

Rotate three times in one direction, then three times in the other direction.

8. Throat Recharging

Tense your whole throat and front of the neck, then relax. Do this three times. Next, tense just the left side of your neck, then relax. Tense just the right side of your neck, then relax.

Do this three times on each side.

9. Neck Recharging

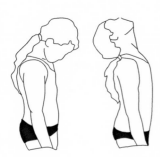

Gently relax your head to your chest. Don't let the head snap down. Then double inhale as you slowly pull your head back up with tension in the back of the neck. Double exhale as you slowly relax the head back down.

Do this three times.

10. Neck Rotation

With medium tension in your neck, rotate your head in small circles.

Repeat three times in one direction, then three times in the other direction.

Repeat the neck rotation with no tension, three times in each direction.

CAUTION: *Don't "grind" the neck or let the head flop around. If you have neck injuries you may want to lift your shoulders up to make this exercise more comfortable for you.*

11. Spinal Recharging *(lower back adjustment)*

Stand with your feet apart, legs straight. Twist your upper body, shoulders, and arms in one direction while you twist your hips and lower body slightly in the opposite direction (a quick yet smooth motion). Your feet should remain stationary, your elbows slightly bent, your fists positioned about hip level, and head pointed forward.

Alternate twisting to the left and right. Twist each way three or more times.

12. Spinal Rotation

Stand with your feet hip-width apart and your hands at your waist. Bend forward at the hips and arch your back slightly. With your hips stationary, and keeping the arch in your back (with low tension in your lower back), rotate your trunk in small circles.

Three times in one direction, then repeat three in the other, relaxing momentarily in between.

13. Spinal Stretching *(from side to side)*

Stand with your feet apart and hands on your hips at your waist. Maintain tension along the spine as you bend your upper body to the left, then to the right. Keep your lower body stationary, including your hips, and keep your head in a straight line with the spine. Move only from the waist upward.

Do this three times.

14. Spinal Adjustment

Place your knuckles or thumbs on the muscles on each side of the base of the spine. Bend slightly forward, then press your hands firmly into your back and arch your spine forward, drawing your head and upper body slightly up and back.

Repeat, working up the spine as high as you can go.

CAUTION: *Do not snap your back in a violent motion. Rather feel the steady pressure of the fists on the back pushing you forward.*

Contact us: course@ananda.org • 530.470.2340

15. Upper Spinal Twisting *(with arms from side to side)*

Stand with your feet apart, arms straight out in front of you at shoulder height, with the fists facing each other. Keeping your hips stationary, twist your upper body and arms from side to side. Hold tension in your arms as you twist; release it at the end of your twist. Keep your leading arm straight and allow the trailing arm to bend at the elbow. Follow your hands with your eyes and head.

Do this three times in each direction.

16. Skull Tapping / Memory Exercise

Briskly rap your skull and forehead all over with your knuckles to stimulate the energy in the brain. Visualize all your brain cells being awakened with cosmic energy.

Do repeatedly covering entire head surface, omitting face and neck.

17. Scalp Massage

Press your fingertips firmly on your head, and rotate small areas of your scalp in circles. Move the scalp over the skull; don't merely rub the head. Push down with your fingers hard enough to feel the skin moving. Then move the fingers on the head to another position.

Continue until you've massaged the entire scalp.

18. Medulla Massage — Medulla Memory Exercise

With the first three fingers of each hand, massage the medulla (the depression at the base of the skull) in small circles: three times in one direction, then three times the other direction. Then double inhale as you arch your head slowly back against the pressure of your fingers, tensing your neck. Double exhale as you relax and gently press your head to your chest with the fingers.

Do this sequence three times.

19. Biceps Recharging

Clasp your hands above your head, or on your head. Tense and relax your left biceps muscles —the muscles in your left upper arm. Then tense and relax your right biceps.

Alternate doing each side three times. Keep the hands relaxed.

20. Twenty-Part Body Recharging

a) Tense the entire body simultaneously. Double inhale and tense your whole body with low, to medium, to high tension. Hold. Then double exhale as you relax completely from high, to medium, to low tension.

b) Tense and relax the twenty body parts individually. Tense each part for about three to four seconds. Begin with the feet—left foot then right. Tense each foot by curling the toes under. Next alternately tense the left calf, then the right calf, being sure to relax each after tensing. Then tense and relax the thighs—left side first then right. Next the buttocks, left and right. Now tense and relax the abdomen below the navel, then the stomach above the navel. Next alternately tense and relax the forearms, then the upper arms, and then the chest. Now tense and relax the four parts of the neck—left, right, front and back. Don't tense suddenly but with low, medium and then high tension, until the body part vibrates.

c) Tense the twenty body parts, holding the tension. Tense these same 20 body parts in the same order, but this time hold the tension as you go. Tense only to medium tension. Inhale as you tense up the body, timing the inhalation to last until you have completely tensed all the body parts. (You will need to move much more quickly than with the individual tension.) When you have finished with the throat, inhale completely and tense to high tension, vibrating all over. Then exhale slowly with a double breath, as you lower the chin to the chest and relax the muscles in the head and neck.

Now continue down the body to relax the other body parts in reverse order until you've completely relaxed your whole body and finished your exhalation. Feel that your body is made of energy.

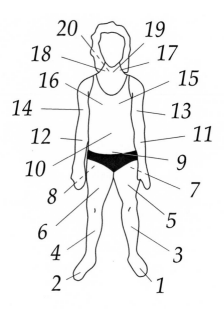

21. Weight Lifting in Front

Stand with your arms at your sides and your hands in fists, palms facing each other. Bend at the elbows and bring the hands up, tensing as though lifting heavy weights. Relax at the top. Push the hands back down, with tension. Relax momentarily at the bottom.

Do this three times.

Optional: Double inhale as you lift the hands, double exhale as you press them down.

22. Double Breathing *(with elbows touching)*

With your arms bent at right angles out to your sides, exhale with a double breath and bring your elbows together, with fists together (palms facing each other) in front. Then inhale with a double breath and tense in a wave as in exercise #1. Here, keep your hands in fists, elbows bent, and upper arms horizontal throughout.

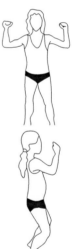

Do this three to five times.

23. Weight Pulling from the Side

Extend your arms straight out to your sides at shoulder level. Clench your fists, with the fists facing up. With tension in the arms, draw the fists toward the head, then relax momentarily. Press the fists away from your head with tension, then relax momentarily.

Do this three times.

Optional: *Double inhale as you bring the arms in, double exhale as you extend them out.*

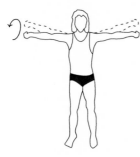

24. Arm Rotation (*in small circles*)

Stand with your arms extended straight out to your sides at shoulder level and your hands in fists, palms facing up. Rotate your arms several times in small circles with increasing tension.

Relax briefly, then repeat in the opposite direction.

25. Weight Pulling from the Front

Begin with the backs of your fists near your forehead with your upper arms parallel to the floor and elbows bent. Extend your arms straight out in front with tension, as if pushing weights. Relax, then pull your hands to your forehead as if pulling weights in. Relax. *Do this three times in each direction.*

Optional: Double inhale as you bring the arms in, double exhale as you extend them out.

26. Finger Recharging

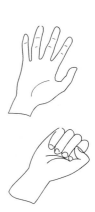

Beginning with your arms at your sides, open and close your hands several times with tension in your hands and fingers: quickly squeeze your hands into fists, then "burst" open your fists. Repeat with your arms straight out to your sides at shoulder height, then straight out in front, and finally extended overhead.

27. Four Part Arm Recharging

Begin with your arms at your sides. Then bring your fists to chest level. Tense your arms and in a continuous motion push the fists out to the side. Then pull them back to the chest and push the arms out to the front. Then return them to the chest and sweep them up above your head, rising up on your toes as you reach full extension. End by coming down off your toes and relaxing the arms, first to your chests and then lowering your hands to your sides. The arms should be tensed throughout these movements, but relaxed momentarily at the points where they are fully extended and when the fists touch the chest. The breathing is as follows: Inhale as you extend the arms from the chest outward to the sides and back to the chest. Exhale with the movement pushing forward and coming back to the chest. Inhale with a double breath as you extend the arms above your head. Finally exhale with a double breath as you relax them down to the waist.

Repeat three times.

step 1   step 2   step 3

step 4   step 5   step 6

step 7   step 8

28. Single Arm Recharging

Stand with both arms down to your sides. Double inhale as you tense your straightened left arm, with hand in a fist, and lift it forward and up over your head (as if you are lifting a weight). Double exhale as you relax the arm back down to your side. Repeat with the right arm.

Alternate doing both sides three times.

Optional: You can rise up onto your toes as you do this.

29. Stretching Side to Side

Stand with both arms down at your sides, and your feet apart. Double inhale as you tense your left arm, with hand in a fist, out to the side and up near your head, (again, as if you are lifting a weight) then continue its swing as you bend your upper body at the waist to your right. Don't let your head drop over to the side; keep it up against the arm. Double exhale as you relax down.

Repeat with the right arm, bending your body to the left. Alternate doing each side three times.

30. Walking in Place

Walk in place with an exaggerated marching step, lifting your knees high (until your thighs are parallel to the floor) and swinging the opposite arm as you march. Try to keep your concentration on the flow of energy; remember that the movement in this exercise is secondary to becoming aware of the energy in the different body parts and sending that energy to those parts that you are moving.

Repeat 25-50 times.

31. Running in Place

Run vigorously in place with a bouncing step, lifting your knees and thighs up high, and if possible, bringing your heels up to strike your buttocks. Do not move the arms but hold your bent elbows steady throughout the exercise.

Repeat 25-50 times.

32. Fencing

Start with both fists at your chest. Double exhale as you step your left foot forward and thrust your right arm forward, tensing the entire right side of your body (as though closing a heavy door). Don't lean forward as you thrust but stay centered over the middle of your body. Double inhale as you step back and relax into the initial position. Repeat to the other side.

Do each side three times, alternating. (Make sure you are extending the opposite arm and leg.)

33. Arm Rotation *(in large circles)*

Double inhale as you swing both of your tensed arms, with hands in fists, behind you and up overhead in large circles. Double exhale as you relax them forward and down. *Do this three times.* Then reverse direction, double inhaling as you swing your tensed arms forward and up, double exhaling as you relax them behind and down.
Do this three times.

34. Stomach Exercise

Exhale fully and bend over slightly, resting the heels of your hands on the tops of
your thighs. Without inhaling, draw your
abdomen strongly toward your spine. Hold.
When needed, relax, straighten up and inhale.

Repeat: This time draw the abdomen in and
push it out, strongly and rhythmically, several times, with breath held out. Repeat once more, or as
an alternative, rotate and churn the abdominal muscles.
(This is a very good exercise for stimulating the digestion and the internal organs.)

35. Double Breathing *(with palms touching)*

Repeat exercise number one.

36. Calf Recharging

Repeat exercise number two.

37. Ankle Rotation

Repeat exercise number three.

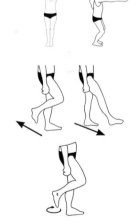

38. Leg Rotation *(hip recharging)*

Standing on your right foot, rotate your straightened left leg in large circles (with your relaxed left foot just clearing the floor). Then reverse, rotating it in the opposite direction. Switch to the opposite leg and repeat. Focus on sending energy to your hip, which this exercise specifically helps.

Rotate each leg three times in each direction.

39. Double Breathing *(without tension)*

With elbows bent and hands in a relaxed fist position facing outward, draw your hands towards your upper chest and shoulder area. Close your eyes and focus your attention at the point between the eyebrows. Softly double exhale as you extend your arms and hands in front, and hold them there. Enjoy the pause between breaths. Softly double inhale as you bring your hands back to your chest. Enjoy that pause as well. Feel relaxed, peaceful, and energized.

Repeat 6-10 times.

Quotes on Energization
From the Yogoda Lessons
By Paramhansa Yogananda
Copyright 1924

"Yogoda [Energization]" teaches how to surround each body cell with a ring of super-charged electrical vital energy and thus keep free from decay of bacterial invasion. It keeps not only the muscles, but all the tissues of the body, bones, marrow, brain, and cells in perfect health."

"Yogoda brings about the growth of all the cells and tissues. It teaches how to recharge the body battery with fresh life current by increasing the will power. It gives specific methods to strengthen and recharge the muscles, not only collectively, but individually, with vital force. It establishes harmony between the working of the voluntary muscles and the involuntary processes. And this harmony gives wonderful health and strength."

"Yogoda causes the resurrection of dying tissue cells and worn out facilities and the formation of billions of new cells and fresh facilities all through the right exercise of will. Through it all the various tissues—bony, muscular, connective, nerve, etc.—are proportionately formed and the mind is strengthened. The circulation, respiration, digestion, and all other involuntary processes of the body are harmonized and invigorated, the mind is clarified."

"Yogoda teaches the art of consciously sending the curative life energy to any diseased body part. By its aid the general vitality of the body is markedly raised, resulting in a wonderful development of tissue, strength, and unexpected nerve vigor, thereby insuring greater longevity. Memory and brain power are also increased through greater blood supply."

Routine

Practice the Energization Exercises either before or after your meditation. Then sit for your meditation and follow your normal routine:

- Pray for grace and guidance.
- Tense and relax (with double breath) three to six times.
- Practice regular breathing for six to twelve rounds.
- Do deep relaxation from toes to head.
- Relax the mind, setting aside all thoughts of past and future.
- Chant, do a visualization, or repeat a deep prayer over several times.
- Practice *Hong-Sau* for a few minutes.
- Attune yourself to God's presence within.
- Stay as long as possible in the inner silence.
- End with a prayer for your loved ones and for the world.

Do This Today

1. Practice the Energization Exercises with the guided DVD.
2. Memorize the first five or six exercises.
3. Order the poster.

Resources to Take You Further

We have aids to help you in learning these important exercises. They are offered as a set and individually.

Wall poster: with the complete descriptions and illustrations.

Audio CD: for those that need an audio reminder on how to do these exercises. Track one has a detailed description of the exercises. Track two is in a "call-out" style of each exercise name to help you through the complete set.

BRINGING MEDITATION INTO DAILY ACTIVITY

Lesson 7

Principles

Make Your Practice Everyday

It is important to bring meditative attitudes into daily life. Unless you are particularly enthusiastic, it is unlikely that you are meditating for more than a small part of each day—an hour or two at most. What about the remaining hours? Are they spiritual tar pits? Unfortunately, many people think so. It is quite common to hear the sentiment, "I can't wait to get off work and back to my spiritual life." Even long-time seekers make the mistake of creating a polarity between their "regular" and "spiritual" lives. But for a successful integrated life, activity and meditation must be brought into proper balance, and both must be spiritualized.

Every wholesome activity is spiritual. God gave us hands and feet, bodies and brains for a purpose. If we can see the hidden divinity behind all outward forms, we will live in a world of wonder and magnificence. But this way of seeing does not come through the senses. We break out of such limitation only by developing an attitude of inner self-offering. Yogananda said it beautifully in this simple poem:

I Was Made for Thee

I was made for Thee alone. I was made for dropping flowers of devotion gently at Thy feet on the altar of the morning.

My hands were made to serve Thee willingly, to remain folded in adoration, waiting for Thy coming; and, when Thou comest, to bathe Thy feet with my tears.

My voice was made to sing Thy glory.

My feet were made to seek Thy temples everywhere.

My eyes were made a chalice to hold Thy burning love and the wisdom falling from Thy nature's hands.

My ears were made to catch the music of Thy footsteps echoing through the halls of space, and to hear Thy divine melodies flowing through all heart-tracts of devotion.

My lips were made to breathe forth Thy praises and Thine intoxicating inspirations.

My love was made to throw incandescent searchlight flames to find Thee hidden in the forest of my desires.

My heart was made to respond to Thy call alone.

My soul was made to be the channel through which Thy love might flow uninterruptedly into all thirsty souls.

All creatures, all people, all life are but extensions of the one Creator. We will have true vision only when we can see unity where others see diversity, when we see God where others see only matter.

Deep meditation gives us expanded awareness, but we can lead daily life in such a way that it, too, will raise our consciousness. One secret is to be aware of how our activities affect our level of consciousness. We constantly exchange energy with everything around us. Improve the quality of that exchange and we will improve the quality of life.

Start by evaluating your immediate environment. It will either enhance or diminish any effort you are making to improve yourself. Yogananda often said, "Environment is stronger than will power."

Look around your living space. Is it uplifting? Is it beautiful? Is it even clean? Messy environments create low vibrations. Once a great yogi, Swami Chidananda, was visiting Ananda Village. As he walked through the garden, he spotted a rusty can lying on the ground.

"What is that used for?" he asked.

"It is a watering can," replied one of the gardeners.

"Then," Chidananda responded, "it should be painted and given its own place. Dirty objects attract lower astral entities."

Your social environment is as important as your physical environment. What kind of friends do you spend your time with? Are they likely to help uplift you or to bring you down? Where do you work? Where do you go for entertainment?

Most of us wouldn't choose to spend time in the company of thieves, murderers, or emotionally unbalanced people. Yet, thoughtlessly, some of us are with such people for hours every day! Be aware of what you watch on TV and at the movies! It has a powerful effect on your consciousness. The same goes for books, magazines, and other sources of entertainment. These are food for your mind. Are you feeding yourself in a way that will make you healthy? If not, change your habits.

Music is one of the most powerful influences of all, because it is pure vibration. Watch very carefully the kind of music you habitually play—it should help lift your spirits. Make sure that it is not egoic or depressing. As we have learned, everything is energy. Be very careful about the quality of the energy in your life.

To change your consciousness, change your environment. Spend time in beautiful places. Be more in nature. And especially spend time in the company of uplifting people. In the teachings of yoga, *satsang* (spending time in the company of other truth-seekers) is the second most powerful influence on the spiritual path. The first is the grace of the guru.

Group meditation is very helpful. Try to find a group of people who meditate regularly. The friendship and encouragement of others who have been meditating longer than you is a very powerful spiritual force. It would be very helpful to join a meditation group. Ananda has over one hundred such groups around the world. For information on groups near you call or write:

Ananda Sangha Worldwide
14618 Tyler Foote Road
Nevada City, CA 95959
530.478.4560
meditationgroups@ananda.org

The most powerful influence of all is to spend time with saints. In the Indian Scriptures it says, "One moment in the company of a saint can be your raft over the ocean of delusion." While it is not always easy to be with a living saint, you can read books by and about those who have found God. Develop this simple habit: Immediately after meditating, spend a few minutes reading spiritual literature. This will not only help connect you to a saintly consciousness but also provide a perfect bridge to outward activity. Before going to bed, you might also read some spiritual literature. It will keep your mind uplifted through the night.

Try also, in other ways, to create a bridge between meditation and activity. Consider the first few minutes of activity to be a continuation of your meditation, a kind of walking meditation. Feel that you are centered physically in your spine and acting from there. Make your movements an extension of the peace you have experienced. Be graceful. Be joyful!

Build short periods of meditation into your daily schedule. Every hour or two take a few minutes to center yourself. If you are with other people, you can simply close your eyes as if you are resting for a few moments. If possible, meditate for a short period before lunch. This will help you stay connected with your inner self. There are a number of practices that can be used to make daily life uplifting

Techniques

Japa

One of the most powerful God-reminding techniques is called *japa* in India, and consists of repeating a *mantra* or prayer throughout the day. You may have seen Buddhist monks fingering their beads and murmuring their great mantra, "Om mani padme hum"—"Om, the jewel in the lotus."

You don't need to do anything that seems foreign to you—simply repeat a prayer or chant, or even just a part of one, as often as possible during the day. Although easy to do, this simple practice can have amazing effects. It fills in idle times with a constantly uplifting force. Over time it will help to gradually reprogram your subconscious mind and wash away worries and negative thoughts.

There is an ancient tradition of repetitive prayer in Christianity. It was a practice of the early desert fathers and has remained a vital teaching in the Greek Orthodox Church. There is a very inspiring book called *The Way of a Pilgrim*, which chronicles the total transformation of an anonymous Russian peasant. One day at church, hearing the words from the Bible, "Pray without ceasing," he became fixed upon a quest to actually achieve this state. He began repeating a simple prayer, "Lord Jesus Christ, have mercy on me." Gradually, as this prayer, known as "the prayer of the heart," began to fill his hours and his thoughts, he formed a living connection with Christ. After many months of effort he realized that it was no longer his tongue or his mind repeating the prayer but rather the very beat of his heart.

Try repeating a simple phrase, such as "I want only Thee, Lord," as often as possible throughout the day. You can do it any time you don't need full concentration on the task at hand. Train yourself to look for opportunities to do your *japa*, such as when you are commuting, or waiting in line, or cooking.

Practicing the Presence of God

Another somewhat similar technique is "practicing the presence of God." Try to feel that you are constantly in the company of Christ or Yogananda or any form of divinity that appeals to you. Bring him, or her (Yogananda used to worship God in the form of Divine Mother), to mind as often as possible. Carry on a silent, inner dialogue with him. Let him be your constant companion. When you eat, eat with him. When you walk or work or play feel him with you. Act as if he is your closest friend.

Gradually try to feel that he is not just beside you, but within you. As you write, feel that it is his hand that moves. As you speak, it is his words, his thoughts that flow through you. As you walk it is his footprints that you leave behind.

It will help if you can keep your consciousness focused at the spiritual eye, between the eyebrows. This is the spot, in our subtle body, where enlightenment takes place. Yogananda said that the light from this source actually changes our brain cells. He taught also that keeping your consciousness here is one of the fastest ways to evolve spiritually.

Journal Writing

It is very helpful to keep a spiritual diary. Feel that you are writing a daily report to your own personal guardian angel. Be completely sincere and totally honest. Report your triumphs and your failures. Chronicle your insights and your progress. Write down important events, both outward and inward. It helps to clarify and focus your thoughts to express them in words.

It is very instructive to look back through your old journals to see what progress you have made.

Review the Day

A similar technique, and a very helpful practice, is to review the day in your evening meditation. Honest self-analysis is very important. Go through the day from morning until evening and review what happened, what you did, what you said. What was the effect of your words and actions on others? If you made mistakes, admit them, inwardly apologize, and pray for help in improving yourself. But don't hold onto your past mistakes or feel guilty. If we didn't make mistakes, we wouldn't need to be in this school of life. Besides, feeling guilty is often just a substitute for making the necessary effort to change yourself.

Those who have had a near-death experience report that a similar "review" happens shortly after we leave the body. In the presence of an entirely benevolent guardian spirit they were given the chance to review their life. They saw and felt events as if they were reliving them with greatly expanded awareness. Not only did they see their actions but saw also the resulting effect on others. Those that were helpful or kind gave them tremendous joy during the life reviews. Those that were harmful caused them deep pain. No one judged them, they simply felt clearly the consequences of their deeds. Many of those who have had a near-death experience come back to life filled with determination to love more deeply, to be a source of kindness and compassion.

Spend a few minutes each evening conducting such a review for yourself. If you had times of confusion, hold the incident up to the light and ask for guidance and clarity. Stand back a bit, as if seeking guidance for a friend rather than for yourself, and ask how you could have done it better. Feel for the answer in your heart—it is the center of intuition. In order to get such guidance, you must be calm and detached. Otherwise you will block or muddy any intuitive perceptions.

Always end the day by totally offering yourself to God. Feel that you are releasing all attachments, all desires, all limiting self-definitions into His light. You can even imagine that each night's sleep is a mini-death. (Yogis in India sometimes meditate in graveyards in order to help break attachment to the body.) Try to feel, before sleep, that you are completely free in your self. Visualize the heart, where attachments form, as a golden ball of light. See desires and attachments as strings attached to this golden globe. Now, cut off every string until the ball is perfectly smooth. Polish the ball, and as you do so, feel that you are becoming freer and freer. Offer everything that you possess and everything that you are back to God, from whence it came. Become one with His light. Try to stay in that state as you drift into sleep, and try to awaken in that infinite freedom as you regain awareness in the morning.

Routine

- Do a few relaxing postures before meditation.
- Meditate at least twice, and preferably three times, per day using the techniques you have learned.
- Practice the Energization Exercises daily.
- Practice the presence of God during the day.
- Review the day in your evening meditation or before sleep.
- Read some spiritual literature every day.

Do This Today

1. Start a spiritual diary.
2. Choose a simple chant or mantra and try repeating it as often as possible.
3. Enjoy yourself more.

Resources to Take You Further

Available as CDs or MP3 downloads:

Mantra, chanted by Kriyananda

AUM: Mantra of Eternity, chanted by Kriyananda

Books:

God Is for Everyone, by Swami Kriyananda

The Way of a Pilgrim, by an Anonymous Pilgrim, Hope Publishing House, 1993

Practicing His Presence, by Lawrence and Laubach, The Seedsowers, 1973

Spiritual Roots

The *Ananda Course in Self-Realization* is based on the teachings of Paramhansa Yogananda, author of the spiritual classic *Autobiography of a Yogi*. Yogananda was the first great Indian master of yoga to make his home in the West. By sharing with countless Americans the life-transforming techniques of yoga and meditation, he opened the door to their own direct experience of spiritual realities.

• • • • • • • •

"As a bright light shining in the midst of darkness, so was Yogananda's presence in this world. Such a great soul comes on earth only rarely, when there is a real need among men."

—The Shankaracharya of Kanchipuram

PARAMHANSA YOGANANDA

Born in India in 1893, Paramhansa Yogananda was trained from his early years to bring India's ancient science of Self-realization to the West. In 1920 he moved to the United States to begin what was to develop into a worldwide work touching millions of lives. Americans were hungry for India's spiritual teachings, and for the liberating techniques of yoga.

In 1946 he published what has become a spiritual classic and one of the best-loved books of the twentieth century, *Autobiography of a Yogi*. In addition, Yogananda established headquarters for a worldwide work, wrote a number of books and study courses, gave lectures to thousands in most major cities across the United States, wrote music and poetry, and trained disciples. He was invited to the White House by Calvin Coolidge, and he initiated Mahatma Gandhi into Kriya Yoga, his most advanced meditation technique.

Yogananda's message to the West highlighted the unity of all religions, and the importance of love for God combined with scientific techniques of meditation.

"Swami Kriyananda is a man of wisdom and compassion in action, truly one of the leading lights in the spiritual world today."

—Lama Surya Das, Dzogchen Center, author of *Awakening The Buddha Within*

Swami Kriyananda

A prolific author, accomplished composer, playwright, and artist, and a world-renowned spiritual teacher, Swami Kriyananda refers to himself simply as "a humble disciple" of the great God-realized master, Paramhansa Yogananda. He met his guru at the young age of twenty-two, and served him during the last four years of the Master's life. And he has done so continuously ever since.

Kriyananda was born in Rumania of American parents, and educated in Europe, England, and the United States. Philosophically and artistically inclined from youth, he soon came to question life's meaning and society's values. During a period of intense inward reflection, he discovered Yogananda's *Autobiography of a Yogi*, and immediately traveled three thousand miles from New York to California to meet the Master, who accepted him as a monastic disciple. Yogananda appointed him as the head of the monastery, authorized him to teach in his name and to give initiation into Kriya Yoga, and entrusted him with the missions of writing and developing what he called "world-brotherhood colonies."

Recognized as the "father of the spiritual communities movement" in the United States, Swami Kriyananda founded the Ananda World Brotherhood Community in the Sierra Nevada Foothills of Northern California in 1968. It has served as a model for seven communities founded subsequently in the United States, Europe, and India.

In 2003 Swami Kriyananda, then in his seventy-eighth year, moved to India with a small international group of disciples, to dedicate his remaining years to making his guru's teachings better known. He appears daily on Indian national television with his program A Way of Awakening. He has established Ananda Sangha Publications, which publishes many of his one hundred literary works and spreads the teachings of Kriya Yoga throughout India. His vision for the next years includes founding cooperative spiritual communities in India (there are two communites now in India, one in Gurgaon and the other in Pune); a temple of all religions dedicated to Paramhansa Yogananda; a retreat center; a school system; a monastery; as well as a university-level Yoga Institute of Living Wisdom.

About the Author

JYOTISH NOVAK has studied, practiced and taught meditation around the world for over forty years. He came onto the spiritual path when he met Swami Kriyananda in 1966. Jyotish was a founding member of Ananda World Brotherhood Village in Nevada City, California in 1968.

During the first ten years, Jyotish served as General Manager of Ananda Village. He and his wife Devi started the first city ashram for Ananda Sangha Worldwide in San Francisco in 1979. In 1984 Jyotish expanded Ananda's outreach and helped start the work in Europe. Jyotish currently serves as the Spiritual Director of Ananda Sangha Worldwide.

Jyotish, who holds a BA in psychology, is the author of the best-selling book *How to Meditate*, along with *30 Day Essentials for Career* and *30 Day Essentials for Marriage*. He also is the creator of *Meditation Therapy*™ and a DVD including these topics: Stress & Change, Relationships, and Health and Healing.

Resources

Books
Published by Crystal Clarity Publishers

Crystal Clarity publishes the **original 1946, unedited edition** of Paramhansa Yogananda's spiritual masterpiece

Autobiography of a Yogi
by Paramhansa Yogananda

Crystal Clarity publishes the original 1946, unedited edition of Paramhansa Yogananda's spiritual masterpiece. This is a new edition, featuring previously unavailable material, of a true spiritual classic, *Autobiography of a Yogi*: one of the best-selling Eastern philosophy titles of all-time, with millions of copies sold, named one of the best and most influential books of the twentieth century.

This highly prized verbatim reprinting of the original 1946 edition is the ONLY one available free from textual changes made after Yogananda's death. Yogananda was the first yoga master of India whose mission was to live and teach in the West. His first-hand account of his life experiences includes childhood revelations, stories of his visits to saints and masters in India, and long-secret teachings of Self-realization that he made available to the Western reader.

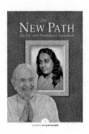

The New Path

My Life with Paramhansa Yogananda

Swami Kriyananda

The New Path tells the story of a young American's spiritual quest, his discovery of the powerful classic, *Autobiography of a Yogi*, and his subsequent meeting with—and acceptance as a disciple by—the book's author, the great spiritual teacher and yoga master, Paramhansa Yogananda.

Swami Kriyananda is an extraordinary narrator: He recreates the vibrancy of his guru's presence, remembers Yogananda's words with perfect clarity, and communicates to the reader the depth of their meaning. Through Kriyananda's eyes and words, you'll be transported into Yogananda's immediate presence as you learn the highest yogic teachings.

The New Path provides a marvelous sequel to Paramhansa Yogananda's own *Autobiography of a Yogi*, helping you to gain a more profound understanding of this great world teacher. Through hundreds of stories of life with Yogananda and through Swami Kriyananda's invaluable insights, you'll discover the inner path that leads to soul-freedom and lasting happiness.

WHAT OTHERS ARE SAYING

"Reading Autobiography of a Yogi *by Paramhansa Yogananda was a transformative experience for me and for millions of others. In* The New Path, *Swami Kriyananda carries on this great tradition. Highly recommended."*

—Dean Ornish, M.D., Founder and President, Preventive Medicine Research Institute, Clinical Professor of Medicine, University of California, San Francisco, author of *The Spectrum*

"Swami Kriyananda has written a compelling and insightful account of his own life, as well as revealing his remembrances of Paramhansa Yogananda. Completely revised and updated, The New Path *is filled with profound reflections, insights, experiences, challenges, and spiritual wisdom. Required reading for every spiritual seeker. I heartily recommend it."*

— Michael Toms, Founder, New Dimensions Media, and author of
True Work and *An Open Life: Joseph Campbell in Conversation with Michael Toms*

"[T]he teaching, the message, and the life of Paramhansa Yogananda are illuminated in a way that makes it possible for us to not only easily access his timeless wisdom, but—through the elegantly easy-to-follow explanations and the living example of one of Master's most devoted disciples—actually apply Eternal Truth to our present-day life. It is impossible for me to think of a greater gift that humanity could receive at this critical time in our evolution as a species, and I am personally and forever grateful to Swamji for this blessed offering."

— Neale Donald Walsch, author of *Conversations with God*

Ananda Yoga for Higher Awareness, by Swami Kriyananda. Contains many of the basic Hatha Yoga postures with their affirmations and illustrations of each pose.

Awaken to Superconsciousness: How to Use Meditation for Inner Peace, Intuitive Guidance, and Greater Awareness, by Swami Kriyananda. A clearly written guide to raising one's awareness out of ordinary consciousness into superconsciousness.

God Is for Everyone, by Swami Kriyananda. This book presents a concept of God and spiritual meaning that will appeal to everyone.

How to Meditate, by Jyotish Novak. A clear and concise guidebook that explains the essential techniques to meditation.

Meditation for Starters, by Swami Kriyananda. A simple book providing what you need to begin a meditation practice.

Other Titles by the Author
Published by Crystal Clarity Publishers

30-Day Essentials™ for Marriage, by Jyotish Novak. A step-by-step guide for establishing a new marriage, revitalizing an existing marriage, or enhancing an already solid one.

30-Day Essentials™ for Career, by Jyotish Novak. This book features inspirational advice, quotations, and practical exercises for each of the qualities necessary for finding, building, and sustaining a successful career.

Meditation Therapy™ DVD, by Jyotish John Novak. Each subject is divided into four parts: an introductory talk, a guided visualization, meditative stillness for intuitive solutions, and affirmations and other practical techniques. This DVD includes:
Relationships
Stress and Change
Health and Healing

Audiobooks, Music, & DVDs

Crystal Clarity's complete catalog of titles is available through our website or from any of the popular online sources.

AUDIOBOOKS

Meditation for Starters, by Swami Kriyananda. A guided meditation and visualization.

Metaphysical Meditations, by Swami Kriyananda. Thirteen guided meditations, based on the mystical poetry of Yogananda, set to a background of well-known and inspiring classical music

MUSIC

Chanting CDs performed by Ananda Kirtan, using harmonium, guitar, tablas, kirtals, and done in a live kirtan style. The titles include:

Bliss Chants
Divine Mother Chants
Power Chants
Peace Chants
Love Chants
Wisdom Chants
Wellness Chants

Mantra CDs chanted by Swami Kriyananda.
  AUM: Mantra of Eternity
  Gayatri Mantra
  Mahamrityanjaya Mantra
  Maha Mantra

DVDs

Yoga for Busy People, by Gyandev McCord and Lisa Powers
Yoga to Awaken the Chakras, by Gyandev McCord
Yoga for Emotional Health, by Lisa Powers

Retreat Centers

The Expanding Light
  14618 Tyler Foote Road, Nevada City, CA 95959
  800.346.5350
  www.expandinglight.org

Ananda Seclusion Retreat
  14618 Tyler Foote Road, Nevada City, CA 95959
  530.292.3024
  www.meditationretreat.org

Energization Exercises Practice Aids

DVD: On track one, Barbara Bingham presents the exercises with detailed instruction. On track two, Swami Kriyananda leads the exercises before a class.

Wall poster: with the complete descriptions and illustrations.

Guided Audio CD: for those that need an audio reminder on how to do these exercises. Track one has a detailed description of the exercises. Track two is in a "call-out" style of each exercise name to help you through the complete set.

Other Recommended Titles

These books are available online or through your favorite bookstore.

The Way of a Pilgrim, by an Anonymous Pilgrim, Hope Publishing House, 1993.

Practicing His Presence, by Lawrence and Laubach, The Seedsowers, 1973.

Breinigsville, PA USA
18 May 2010
238202BV00001B/1/P